DIRTY
FINGERNAILS

A ONE-OF-A-KIND COLLECTION OF GRAPHICS UNIQUELY DESIGNED BY HAND

JOHN FOSTER

ROCKPORT

© 2009 Rockport Publishers, Inc.

First published in the United States of America by

Rockport Publishers, a member of Quayside Publishing Group

100 Cummings Center, Suite 406-L, Beverly, Massachusetts 01915

Telephone: (978) 282-9590

Fax: (978) 283-2742

www.rockpub.com

Library of Congress Cataloging-in-Publication Data

Foster, John, 1971-

Dirty fingernails : a one-of-a-kind collection of graphics uniquely designed by hand / John Foster.

   p. cm.

ISBN-13: 978-1-59253-552-1

ISBN-10: 1-59253-552-6

1. Commercial art. 2. Graphic design (Typography) I. Title.

NC997.F68 2009

741.6--dc22

2009014432

CIP

ISBN-13: 978-1-59253-552-1

ISBN-10: 1-59253-552-6

10 9 8 7 6 5 4 3 2 1

Design: John Foster, Bad People Good Things LLC

Printed in Singapore

Special thanks to:

My enormous and ever-growing family, especially Suzanne and Lily! Winnie Prentiss, Emily Potts, David Martinell, and everyone at Rockport Publishers. Svetlana Legetic, Cale Charney, and everyone at BYT. Many people inspired me more than they know during the writing of this book: Lexie Moreland, Vaughan Oliver, Jeff Kleinsmith, Robynne Raye, Debbie Millman, Stefan Bucher, Colin Newman, Michael Kentoff, Bill Vierbuchen, Dave Bradbury, Chad Lafley, Rich Westbrook, and many more I am forgetting—you all have a terribly long and ridiculously wet kiss from me in your immediate future.

DIRTY
FINGERNAILS

A ONE-OF-A-KIND COLLECTION OF GRAPHICS UNIQUELY DESIGNED BY HAND

JOHN FOSTER

ROCKPORT PUBLISHERS

PARTICIPATING FIRMS FROM AROUND THE GLOBE

AOOLEU
BAD PEOPLE GOOD THINGS
BANKERWESSEL
ANA BENAROYA
S.BRITT
SCOTT CAMPBELL
FRANCOIS CASPAR
ART CHANTRY DESIGN CO.
THE DECODER RING DESIGN CONCERN
DIRTY PICTURES
NATE DUVAL DESIGN
EL JEFE DESIGN
ODED EZER
HENDERSONBROMSTEADART
FONS HICKMANN M23
MORGAN GUEGAN
HATCH DESIGN
JAMES HEIMER
ZACH HOBBS
INVISIBLE CREATURE
JEWBOY CORPORATION
KWERTY
LEDOUXVILLE
YANN LEGENDRE
RON LIBERTI
THE LITTLE FRIENDS OF PRINTMAKING
LOVELY MPLS
ELLEN LUPTON

MODERN DOG
MORNING BREATH, INC.
MOUNT PLEASANT
NATHANIEL MURPHY
THE NEW YEAR
GUILLAUME NINOVE
NOTHING: SOMETHING: NY
PATENT PENDING DESIGN
AXEL PEEMOELLER
SAGMEISTER, INC.
SANDSTROM DESIGN
NATALIE SCHAEFER DESIGN
DENNY SCHMICKLE DESIGN
SERIPOP
THE SMALL STAKES
SOMMESE DESIGN
SUB POP RECORDS
SUSSNER DESIGN CO.
THINKMULE
TRIP PRINT PRESS
UNDERCONSIDERATION
JAY VOLLMAR
WEATHERMAKER PRESS
JOANNA WECHT DESIGN
MARTIN WOODTLI
YOKOLAND
ZITYPE WORKSHOP

$100.0
It contain
typewrite
printing p
sight from
it the mos
and clean

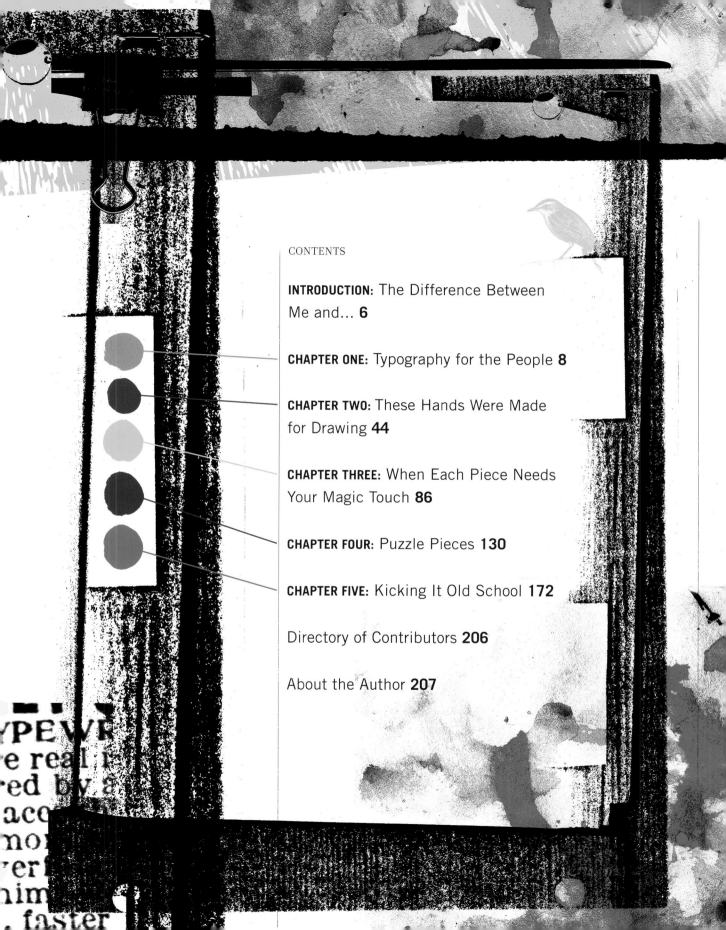

CONTENTS

INTRODUCTION: The Difference Between Me and... **6**

CHAPTER ONE: Typography for the People **8**

CHAPTER TWO: These Hands Were Made for Drawing **44**

CHAPTER THREE: When Each Piece Needs Your Magic Touch **86**

CHAPTER FOUR: Puzzle Pieces **130**

CHAPTER FIVE: Kicking It Old School **172**

Directory of Contributors **206**

About the Author **207**

photo by Lexie Moreland

THE DIFFERENCE

BETWEEN ME AND ...

The computer is a wonderful tool, but it is only that: a tool. Your brain is what your clients are truly paying for and what offers unique qualities found nowhere else. Our hands are the extension of our minds that brings our ideas to fruition. It stands to reason that the closer we can bring the execution of our work to the fireworks in our heads, the closer the work will be to the original thought. This is a given, but it is also the unknown quality of designing in this fashion that is the key. We control the computer, and it rarely creates something out of thin air. The action of our hands, however, often causes happy little accidents and experiments that are not possible digitally.

I advocate reveling in those nuances and unique qualities. We can all choose the same font for a project, but we could never draw identical typography. Clients can see your mode of thinking quickly when this work is available, and your value is increased because they cannot get the same imagery or solution elsewhere. For certain projects, this is just smart business.

For designers, it means even more.

There is a line of thinking that design in the United States returned to a hand-crafted feel as a response to 9/11, and the new millennium has seen a return to this "safe" way of working as designers discovered (or rediscovered, in some cases) the joys and rewards of getting their hands dirty and actually creating something. Even new designers—those who were educated to design on the computer only—are discovering that handmade design, like street art, is more profound and personally satisfying to produce than computer-generated art. The closer relationship of designer to work fosters better, more individual results.

This approach yields work that hits the viewer faster and deeper—work that connects. The work is far from style over substance; the designer's fingerprints are more evident. Whether manifesting directly in the imagery or in the method used to complete the circle—letterpress or silkscreen printing—or, more subtly, as when Stefan Sagmeister builds type and images from patterns of multiple objects and then photographs them, design is more personalized than ever.

Now, designers in Europe, Asia, and South America have joined the ranks of purveyors of hand-drawn type and imperfect photography and illustration. Designers in Mexico and Cuba have continued a long-held tradition of this type of execution, but now we see it cropping up in Germany and the United Kingdom, where the computer and the invisible grid long reigned unopposed.

We are tactile creatures, and we work in an arena where passion and creativity are supreme. We often do this because of an abstract need to create, but when we get the opportunity to physically design with our hands, we realize the need is not abstract but rather direct and tangible. The computer era caused a gulf to form as designers did little other than punching keys or fidgeting with a mouse. They lost touch with their work—literally.

No longer—let's get dirty!

CHAPTER ONE

TYPOGRAPHY FOR THE PEOPLE

In an era when all designers have thousands of fonts at their fingertips, there seems only one way to cut through the logjam: Do it yourself. Nothing irks me more than seeing a type treatment for a corporate identity or an entertainment property—knowing how important it is for those entities to speak in a unique voice—rendered in a font straight off the shelf that any competitor can use the day after its unveiling. It nullifies the power and influence of the identity before it has a chance to embed in the viewer's consciousness. But it simply doesn't have to be that way! The examples in this chapter illustrate the best of hand-rendered type using all types of media. Step back from the computer and explore the limitless possibilities of creating type by hand.

Firm: Sandstrom Design

Title: Be Mine

Designer, illustrator, copywriter:

Steve Sandstrom

Size: 7 × 7 inches (17.8 × 17.8 cm)

Materials: Found wooden stick,

India ink, mat board

Printing process: Hand-lettering

"I psyched myself into a frenzy before I wrote the lines," confesses Steve Sandstrom. "I found a stick and dipped it into ink as a crude quill pen, which ran out of ink quickly as it was dragged across the paper. I retraced certain letters more than once to get them to become complete letterforms. Somewhat randomly, I determined that every S would be drawn over itself eighteen times. Every S, eighteen times. Every S, eighteen times," he repeats, like a mantra. "This piece was done as a specific hand-lettering style for a Nike campaign by Wieden+Kennedy that was art directed by John Boiler. It featured a deranged football referee played by Dennis Hopper. Hopper's line, 'Bad things, man,' was a constant in the campaign. John wanted the lettering to look inspired by outsider art. It ran in television spots during the Super Bowl, and the lettering was utilized for outdoor, print, and point-of-sale executions." But Sandstrom wasn't done yet. "Because Valentine's Day was coming up, I used the same lettering technique and approach to make an equally disturbing and threatening valentine for my girlfriend. She's my wife now—as if she really had any choice in the matter. Bad things, man."

Firm: Ana Benaroya

Title: Slickee Boys

Designer, illustrator: Ana Benaroya

Size: 11 × 17 inches (27.9 × 43.2 cm)

Materials: India ink, Photoshop

Printing process: Digital print

"All I really needed was the name of the head-lining band and I was ready to go," says Ana Benaroya with a smile. "I pictured a scruffy rocker with long, flowing locks slicking his hair back. I wanted the text to mimic the hair, so I had some words and lines flow into each other. Once again, this poster was one that I pieced together from different drawings. In Photoshop, I do a lot of painting and then erasing to carve shapes out. Sometimes working subtractively can be very rewarding." The hand-lettering perfectly complements Benaroya's illustration. "I would always rather hand-draw all my lettering than use a typeface. I feel as though the letters are part of my illustration. I wouldn't want someone else drawing my drawing, so I don't want someone else designing my letters!"

Firm: Ana Benaroya

Title: King Lear

Designer, illustrator: Ana Benaroya

Size: 13 × 19 inches (33 × 48.3 cm)

Materials: India ink, Photoshop

Printing process: Digital printing

"This poster was an instance where the drawing was whole before I scanned it in," explains Ana Benaroya. "Certain elements in the coloring were added afterward in Photoshop, but the composition was already predetermined. I tried to think of broad, general themes that ran through the play, and I focused on betrayal—not seeing things and people as they truly are—and also the aging process." She was determined to illustrate something raw, rather than a scene-specific event, in order to be powerful. "I think most Shakespeare plays call for handcrafted elements. The plays are always basic in their lessons yet extreme in how they are portrayed and acted. So much humanity must be conveyed—and only the hand can do that."

Firm: Fons Hickmann m23

Title: Red Dot: Yearbook of Communication Design

Art directors: Fons Hickmann, Markus Büsges

Designers: Markus Büsges, Fons Hickmann,
André Müller, Thomas Schrott

Photographer: Thomas Schrott

Size: Various

Materials: Cardboard, glue, adhesive tape

Printing process: Offset, photoprinting

In creating the look for the Red Dot annual, Fons Hickmann and team knew they needed to create something amazing to have even a chance of competing with the incredible work in the book. The concept would require a lot of hands to execute as well! "It needed four designers, twelve students, one photographer, one location scout, and four weeks of work," he marvels. "The Red Dot book always gets special attention in terms of design because it is a kind of mother ship of the design family in that it brings together the best work of the year. Therefore it is not always easy to stay cool," he laughs. "The concentration of high-quality design and expertise that comes together in the Red Dot, in the jury as well as the winners, is remarkable. I hope we have once again done a good job. And I can confirm that the enjoyment we have doing this project is higher than the stress factor involved—which is the golden rule behind our work," he smiles.

POSTER BY THE LITTLE FRIENDS OF PRINTMAKING

OCT 03	SEATTLE, WA	OCT 26	READING, PA	NOV 03	BUFFALO, NY
OCT 05	PORTLAND, OR	OCT 27	NEW YORK, NY	NOV 04	CLEVELAND, OH
OCT 06	LOS ANGELES, CA	OCT 28	PHILADELPHIA, PA	NOV 05	LOUISVILLE, KY
OCT 10	SAN DIEGO, CA	OCT 30	PITTSBURGH, PA	NOV 06	BLOOMINGTON, IN
OCT 11	LAS VEGAS, NV	NOV 01	CHICAGO, IL	NOV 08	MINNEAPOLIS, MN
OCT 25	BOSTON, MA	NOV 02	ANN ARBOR, MI	NOV 30	SAN FRANCISCO, CA

Firm: James Heimer

Title: Why?

Art director: Sean Agnew

Designer, illustrator: James Heimer

Size: 11 × 17 inches (27.9 × 43.2 cm)

Materials: Pen, India ink, collage pieces

Printing process: Screenprinting

Inspired by "a combination of Polish movie posters and the band's lyrical content," James Heimer went with a powerful large face while working in a winding snake to encapsulate the complex and at times sinister vibe running throughout Why's lyrical output.

Firm: The Little Friends of Printmaking

Title: The Comedians of Comedy 2007 Tour Poster

Art director: Henry Owings

Designers, illustrators: The Little Friends of Printmaking

Size: 19 × 25 inches (48.3 × 63.5 cm)

Materials: Spray paint, software

Printing process: Screenprinting

"The Comedians of Comedy are forever compared to rock musicians by lazy copywriters, for reasons both tenuous and concrete. They're alternative comedians. They go on tour, they hang out with rock types, and they wear T-shirts and look scruffy," says Melissa Buchanan of The Little Friends. "Our concept was to lampoon their rock connection by showing a tattooed roadie onstage in an obnoxiously complicated metal-style T-shirt that held most of the tour details. They liked the design so much that they asked us to adapt the roadie's shirt into an actual tour shirt, which they sold as merchandise. We're fond of our technique of using found halftone textures, but sometimes we need something that looks softer and a little more random, and that's when we'll use spray paint. We just spray onto paper, goof around with the size and spacing of dots or try to make the paint drip, and then scan it into the computer. There's quite a bit of spray-paint texture in this one. It's easy to pick out once you know it's there."

▶ **Firm:** underconsideration

Title: Lorraine Wild: Full Stride

Designer: Armin Vit

Size: 22 × 34 inches (55.9 × 86.4 cm)

Materials: Light table, Sharpie pens, software

Printing process: Offset

Armin Vit says of his design for a poster for an upcoming lecture by Lorraine Wild, "I wanted to reflect Lorraine's work in book design, an inherently tactile and physical experience. For some reason I also thought it would be funny—at least to me—to have a litany of tiny sentences that all rhymed with Lorraine's last name. So I decided to do something hand-drawn but still tied to the smoothness of the computer, and just let the text take center stage. I set Clarendon in the computer, printed at half-size, and then just retraced it with a Sharpie. The background is an 11 × 17-inch (27.9 × 43.2 cm) piece of paper fully blacked out in Sharpie. Then I scanned it back in, autotraced it in Photoshop, exported to Illustrator, and watched my Apple G5 crawl at a snail's pace trying to deal with all the vectors," he smiles. This process allowed Vit to incorporate the idiosyncrasies he desired, despite his admission that " I cannot illustrate to save my life."

▲ **Firm:** James Heimer

Title: The Progress (#4)

Art directors: Mike Pelone, Bob Meadows

Designer, illustrator: James Heimer

Size: 11 × 17 inches (27.9 × 43.2 cm)

Materials: Pen, India ink, acrylic paint, photocopied collage pieces

Printing process: Screenprinting

Sometimes becoming immersed in your subject matter allows you to unconsciously solve the problem at hand. James Heimer "listened to the band on repeat again and again before making this stream-of-consciousness doodle." He also benefited from the production process while "reclaiming some of my old screens for printing, I ended up with some old chunks of emulsion in the pink screen, which added a little extra grit to it. A happy accident," he smiles.

Sweet Child
Love is Blind
Tongue Tied
Stock Piled
Deep Fried
Please Unwind
Tour Guide
Sun Dried
Dined and Wined
Girls Gone Mild
Rising Tide
Comic Sans, Reviled
Death is Fine
Taxes Filed
Worlds Collide
Step Aside
Bright Side
Bona Fide
California Pride

Lorraine Wild:
Full Stride

Thursday, November 10 at 6:30 p.m. Be there or be digital.

Firm: Sagmeister, Inc.

Title: Keeping a Diary

Art director: Stefan Sagmeister

Designers: Matthias Ernstberger, Stephan Walter

Producers: Joanna Lee, Bert Tan

Creative director: Richard Johnson

Editor: Elena Ho

Size: Various

Materials: Everything we could find!

Printing process: Film

"We were invited to Singapore to produce an installment for the series I developed called 'Things I Have Learned in My Life So Far,' with sponsorship assistance from MDA Singapore," explains Stefan Sagmeister. "This one-minute clip about the importance of keeping a diary was shot in one day in an abandoned historic Tang Dynasty park in Singapore." These stills allow us to see how Sagmeister adapted what had been a still photography exercise into a short movie.

Keeping A Diary images continued through page 20.

Firm: Oded Ezer

Title: Tybrid

Art director, designer, photographer:

Oded Ezer

Size: 19.5 × 19.5 inches (49.5 × 49.5 cm)

each panel

Materials: Paper, metal wires

Printing process: Plotter printout

Oded Ezer's *Tybrid* consists of four squares (each 19.5 × 19.5 inches) combined to form the Hebrew word for *typography*. "I created this for an invitational poster exhibition called My Favorite Game. It first took place in Ithaca, New York, in July 2007, and then the exhibit traveled to Athens, Greece," he explains. "In this work, I have dealt with formal intersections between traditional Hebrew letters and various object silhouettes, consciously ignoring logical context. Using beautiful vector silhouettes from Stefan Gandl's book, and the popular Frankrühl Hebrew typeface, I freely and intuitively released myself from ergonomic and functional restrictions, using methods and materials developed in some of my former experimental works. This poster series is also influenced by Dadaist works and contemporary virtual hybridizations of animals and human beings. This work is a suggestion for typographic visual expression—something to look at and not necessarily to write with. It has always seemed to me that the 3-D design of letters is a logical expansion of traditional 2-D type design."

Firm: Sagmeister, Inc.

Title: Having guts always works out for me.

Art director: Stefan Sagmeister

Designers: Matthias Ernstberger, Miao Wang, Stefan Sagmeister

Photographer: Bela Borsodi

Size: 9 × 11.5 inches (22.9 × 29.2 cm)

Materials: Everything we could find!

Printing process: Offset

Tackling the dividing spreads for Austrian magazine *Copy* once again, Sagmeister and crew set out to capture another empowering phrase. "This time we built the typography in wildly different ways and locations [for photographer Bela Borsodi to capture], and showed a sort of before-and-after effect. The final phrase was *Having guts always works out for me.*"

Having guts always works out for me. Images continued through page 27.

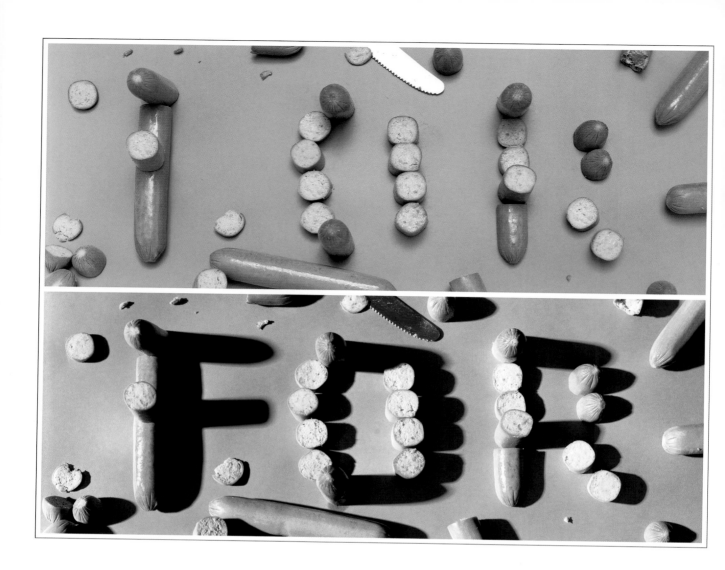

Firm: Oded Ezer

Title: Temporary Type

Art director, designer, photographer: Oded Ezer

Size: Various

Materials: Used industrial air conditioner filters

Printing process: Photography

"In this set, I used old air conditioner filters to create these crumbled letters with a special look, as if they were made of ashes or dust," explains Oded Ezer. "I'm testing the intersection of typography and art. They have meaning, but they are not a medium for direct communication."

Firm: Oded Ezer

Title: I (Heart) Milton

Art director, designer: Oded Ezer

Photographer: Idan Gil

Size: 38.75 × 26.75 inches (98.4 × 67.9 cm)

Materials: Paper

Printing process: Offset

"This is my homage to Milton Glaser's I [heart] NY logo," explains Oded Ezer. "Glaser's design is simple and direct, and I felt it would be recognizable even if I made it more complicated. Coming back from Typo Berlin, I realized how few experimental works I had created in English in the last few years. I saw the enthusiasm of the audience when I showed a single piece in English, so I decided to start a series of homages to [non-Israeli] designers I admire, and of course Milton Glaser is top on that list. I wanted this image to be monumental, mysterious, and intensive."

Firm: Oded Ezer

Title: Tortured Letters

Art director, designer, photographer: Oded Ezer

Size: Various

Materials: Strings, industrial rubber, wood, paper

Printing process: Photography

Oded Ezer set out to apply his magical typographical sculptures to replicate the tragedy of "war crimes and human nature," and he knew he needed to provide the most authentic approach possible. His letterforms are placed in "torturous" positions by his own hands and then photographed.

Firm: Oded Ezer

Title: Open

Art director, designer, photographer: Oded Ezer

Size: 27.5 × 19.75 inches (69.9 × 50.2 cm)

Materials: Paper, old magazines

Printing process: Plotter printout

"I produced this poster for a brand design company named OPEN T.B.E.," says Oded Ezer. Showing how important the photographic aspect of capturing his creation is, "I printed the word *open*, and then cut some parts of it on top of a magazine cover, pulling the edges out—as if it were blown in the wind, revealing the inside parts of the letters to get the desired effect," he says.

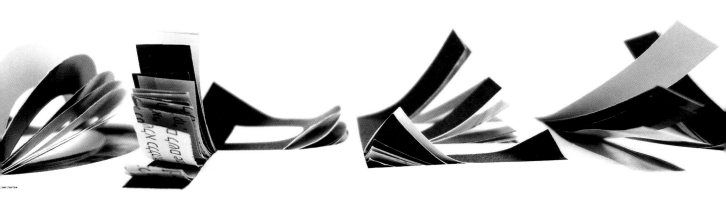

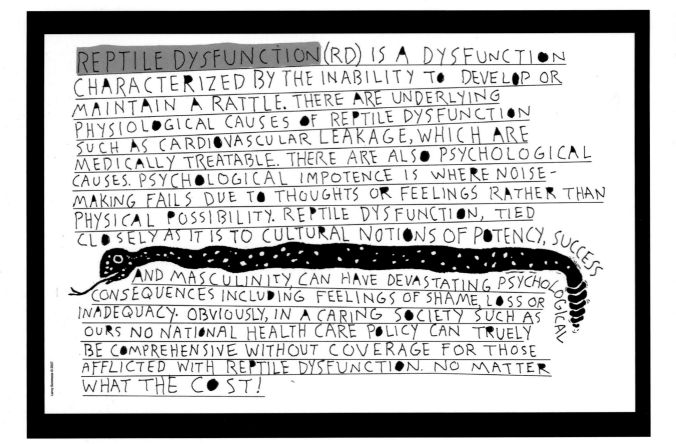

Firm: Sommese Design

Title: Reptile Dysfunction

Designer, illustrator: Lanny Sommese

Size: 24 × 18 inches (61 × 45.7 cm)

Materials: Ink, found art

Printing process: Screenprinting

"This poster was a tongue-in-cheek response to two things," says Lanny Sommese. "The presidential candidates, who appear to be promising everything to everyone to get votes, and the environmentalists, who often make asps out of themselves protecting little hapless wiggly critters. My thought was that unfortunate dysfunctional reptiles should be added to their lists. Why not? Everything else is there with little or no regard for what it will cost the American taxpayers. My goal is to completely obliterate reptile dysfunction in the United States by next Thursday! The idea came to me as I was driving to work listening to the radio. A political ad was followed by an ad for erectile dysfunction elixir. I laughed because the announcers' pronunciation of *erectile* sounded like *reptile*. Initially, I had other copy in mind for the poster. However, when I went to the dictionary and read the definition of *erectile dysfunction*, it was perfect. I used it almost verbatim, substituting *rattle* and *noisemaking* for the erection stuff, and adding the tongue-in-cheek bit at the end. The actual image of the snake was a combination of something I found in an old book on primitive art and my own drawings, combined with my hand-lettering."

Firm: Sagmeister, Inc.

Title: Trying to look good limits my life

Art director: Stefan Sagmeister

Designers: Stefan Sagmeister, Matthias Ernstberger

Size: Five billboards

Materials: Everything we could find!

Printing process: Installation

"The title of this work (and its content) is among the few things I have learned in my life so far," explains Stefan Sagmeister. "Broken into five parts, *Trying to look good limits my life* was displayed in sequence as typographic billboards in Paris for Art Grandeur Nature. They work like a sentimental greeting card left in the park."

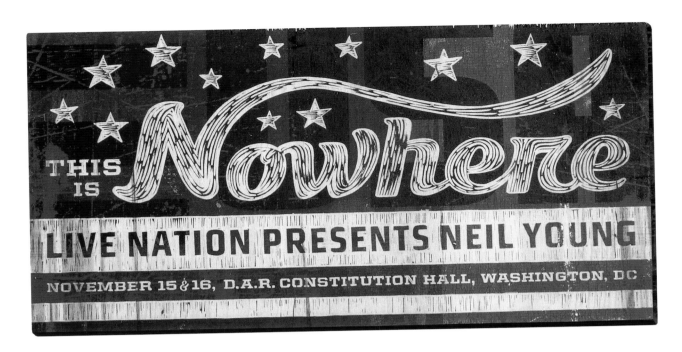

Firm: The Decoder Ring Design Concern

Title: Neil Young Commemorative Poster

Designers: Christian Helms, Geoff Peveto

Size: 22 × 28 inches (55.9 × 71.1 cm)

Materials: Ink, wood

Special production techniques: Hand-distressing

Printing process: Screenprinting, wood engraving

"Neil Young has a particularly sharp political viewpoint," explains Christian Helms, "and his concert was being held in Washington, D.C. Geoff really wanted to do some sort of distressed signage for the piece, and I wanted the poster to be political. We met in the middle with Young's lyric 'This is nowhere' hand-rendered over government signage." For the actual production, "the base elements were screenprinted onto board, and then the display text was etched directly into the wood. Geoff added some hand-distressing to finish the piece," says Helms.

Firm: Sagmeister, Inc.

Title: Everything I do always comes back to me.

Art director: Stefan Sagmeister

Designers: Eva Hueckmann, Matthias Ernstberger, Doris Pesendorfer, Stefan Sagmeister

Photographer: Matthias Ernstberger

Model maker: Eva Hueckmann

Size: 9 × 11.5 inches (22.9 × 29.2 cm)

Materials: Everything we could find!

Printing process: Offset

Stefan Sagmeister explains how the firm created six double page spreads for the Austrian magazine *Copy*. "These are dividing spaces, each opening a new chapter in the magazine. Every month the magazine commissions a new studio to do the design. When our turn came, we started with backgrounds found in clothing wholesalers and from one of our clients, wallpaper company Wolf-Gordon (for "everything" and "to me"). Then we found objects to make the type from butchers and grocery and hardware stores in Chinatown. Together they read, *Everything I do always comes back to me*. Going through the process of finding so many things, we eventually found ourselves."

THESE ARE POWERS

9/20

bottletree

Firm: Zach Hobbs

Title: Skybucket Showcase

Designer, illustrator: Zach Hobbs

Size: 18 × 12 inches (45.7 × 30.5 cm)

Materials: Ink, Xerox, software

Printing process: Digital

For this piece, I just started drawing and let it happen," explains Zach Hobbs. "The show was a label showcase for a good friend of mine who owns Skybucket Records in Birmingham, Alabama. Usually he just lets me go and I try to come up with something fun. However, including so many bands can be a typographical nightmare—all those names, no real headliner. So I just went with it and let my pen do most of the work. I drew the head and the type together as one, and then just split things up into different colors. Easy! The hand holding the cigarette actually came from some old magazine. Once I had the face and hand holding the cigarette together in the layout, it really reminded me of all those fakers and poseurs at every single rock show, standing around smoking and trying to look cool. It wasn't meant to be a slam, but I get a little chuckle every time I see the poster."

Firm: Zach Hobbs

Title: These Are Powers

Designer, illustrator: Zach Hobbs

Size: 20 × 26 inches (50.8 × 66 cm)

Materials: Ink, Xerox, software

Printing process: Screenprinting

"I went for classic gnarly for this band poster but was seriously going for Old Polish Poster in the end, so that inspired the type and layout," says Zach Hobbs. "I have this little trick when I'm working my day job. I'm usually waiting on things to scan or making .pdf files, and I have little bits of dead time. I have a stack of Post-It notes I doodle on while I wait. So many posters have come from these little drawings. You can rely on this: Draw something really, really small and then enlarge it on a photocopier (not one of those new digital jobs). The results vary, but if you do this enough times you will get something cool out of it," he smiles.

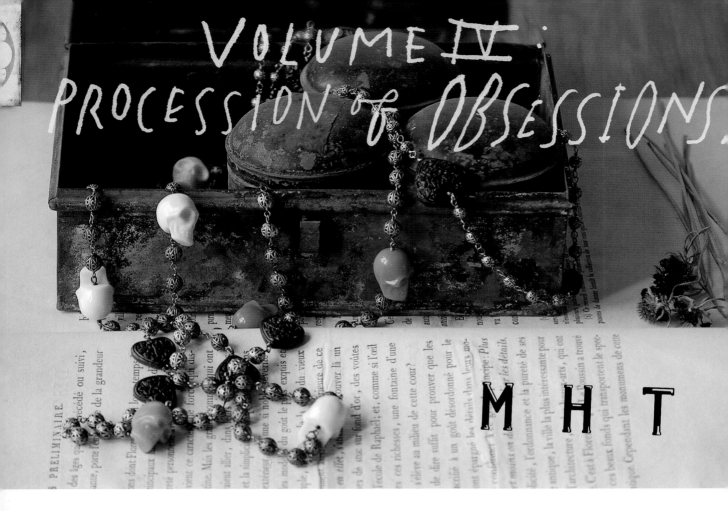

VOLUME IV:
PROCESSION OF OBSESSIONS

MHT

Firm: Nothing: Something: NY

Title: Made Her Think Volume IV:
Procession of Obsessions

Art director, designer: Kevin Landwehr

Photographers: Carlo Van De Roer,
Devin Becker (production)

Size: 8.5 × 5.5 inches (21.6 × 14 cm)

Materials: Ink, found objects

Printing process: Offset

"The ideal of joy in both life and death underlies the dark allure of Made Her Think, a prolific and imaginative jewelry collection by designer Meredith Kahn. Her deeply romantic vision is rich with multifaceted symbols telling unique stories about life and love, and we wanted to design a book that reflects that," explains Kevin Landwehr. "After inspecting and logging every item in her extensive collection, we were impressed by how intensely unique and personal each item felt, so we set about creating a backstory based on snippets of writing from Meredith's journals and thoughts we collected during our many meetings. All of this preceded our photo shoot, which allowed us to carefully choreograph the page-to-page experience. Using the poetry of the dead, we created a romance among objects, allowing the buyers to create a personal connection to the jewelry. As Meredith says, 'Sometimes people are drawn to objects that tell a story. They may not even know it—it just speaks to them.'"

have no FEAR
of a life forever
BLIND.

YOU shall
REST

ou SHALL WAKE
think it SWEET,
that thy love
is NEAR & KIND.

OPPOSITE: 1. Candy Skull Hooks - white, 3"

Meredith Kahn PRESENTS

MADE HER THINK

VOLUME IV

PREVIOUS:
1. Skull Feather Hooks, 3"
2. Shield to Heart Toggle, 21"
THIS PAGE:
1. Candy Skull Strand - white, 6"

Firm: Yokoland

Title: 3.0

Designers, illustrators: Aslak Gurholt Rønsen, Espen Friberg

Photographer: Morten Spaberg

Size: 4.75 × 4.75 inches (12 × 12 cm)

Materials: Bricks, pen

Printing process: Offset

Continuing a sequence of covers for the duo's record label, Metronomicon Audio, designers Aslak Gurholt Rønsen and Espen Friberg constructed volumes 1.0 and 2.0 out of beads and Legos respectively. It seemed inevitable that volume 3.0 would reach this point. "We wanted to build the numbers using bigger parts each time, and bricks just seemed the natural next step," explains Rønsen.

Firm: Axel Peemoeller

Title: Das Spiel Ist Aus

Designer, illustrator: Axel Peemoeller

Size: 16.5 × 11.75 inches (41.9 × 29.9 cm)

Materials: Paint

Printing process: Offset

Designer Axel Peemoeller sat reading the manuscript for the upcoming issue of *Feld* magazine and pondering its focus. "The pages were from a book by Jean-Paul Sartre, *Les Jeux Sont Faits* ('The Game Is Up'), dealing with the subject of life and death. Even with the cover title drawing on the game aspect, I knew I wanted to focus on the severe presentation of life and death when I picked up my paintbrush." The resulting striking image perfectly hits the target.

Firm: Thinkmule

Title: Stationary Odyssey CD

Art directors: Aaron Tanner, Jeremy Pruitt

Designer: Aaron Tanner

Illustrator: Jeremy Pruitt

Size: 5 × 5 inches (12.7 × 12.7 cm)

Materials: Pen, colored pencil, marker

Printing process: Offset

"Stationary Odyssey is the musical endeavor of Indiana natives Aaron Tanner and Brett Siler," explains Jeremy Pruitt. "They have a distinctive mission with their music, and it is not mass consumption. The music has the honesty of folk but the explosiveness of experimental rock. I guess when we were working on the project we thought of it as a journey," he says. "We paid homage to old-school travel but worked in some creatures as well. Because their music doesn't fit into a category we could do whatever we wanted, including mixing in found objects, antiquing backgrounds, and doing pencil drawings."

"I'M VOTING FOR LESS DEPENDENCE ON OIL, & A CLEANER ENVIRONMENT."
-PETER C, NEW YORK NY

"I'M VOTING BECAUSE THE FUTURE WON'T RUN ON OIL."
-DANIEL B, HUNTINGTON BEACH CA

"I'M VOTING TO END A FOOLISH WAR."
-RUSSELL S, CANTON, MA

Firm: The Decoder Ring Design Concern

Title: Barack Obama Campaign: Vote for Change

Art director: Peter Cortez

Designer, illustrator: Christian Helms

Size: Various

Materials: Pen, brush, pencil

Printing process: Offset

Given forty eight hours to make a poster series for the Barack Obama U.S. presidential campaign, Christian Helms leaped at the chance. "These posters are directly inspired by the reasons young voters gave to interviewers when asked to make their voices heard. These are real, honest quotes from real Americans who were pissed off and tired of the direction we were headed for the past eight years. It was important that the work look like it came from a person, not a computer," he stresses. "Viewers connect in a different and deeper way with work that shows involvement of the human hand. That seemed a necessity, considering the subject matter."

CHAPTER TWO

THESE HANDS
WERE MADE FOR
DRAWING

Many designers carry sketchbooks wherever they go, capturing the little things in life that most people take for granted or completely disregard—from the architecture of a building to the smirking smile of a stranger across the room. They draw to pass the time on the train or bus to work or while talking on the phone. Often, these doodles end up being the inspiration for client projects, and that personal touch comes through in the final product. The creative mind solves problems when left to its own devices! Handmade touches give projects a unique voice in the market and can emerge from one source only. What is more amazing than that?

Firm: Ana Benaroya

Title: Hair Together

Designer, illustrator: Ana Benaroya

Size: 17 × 11 inches (43.2 × 27.9 cm)

Materials: India ink, software

Printing process: Digital print

"I was once given a fortune cookie and told to illustrate the fortune inside, which read, 'You show your true face to those who really matter.' After several literal sketches and attempts, I went for a more whimsical approach and got what I was looking for," explains Ana Benaroya. The final illustration "would be humorous if it had a couple with hair covering their faces, thereby hiding their faces both from the viewer and from each other. Each part was actually drawn separately and then pieced together digitally. I work this way often because it gives me more flexibility when composing a piece. I can add and take away an element very easily. Even though this piece is very graphic—as is most of my work—I always like to begin with a painting. The line work is all done with a brush and India ink, and I think that gives the couple real vitality. The line has a flow that I don't think could be achieved in a purely digital realm." The final art was later used as a cover for the Seattle newspaper *The Stranger*. "It's great when a client wants your personal work!" Ana exclaims.

Firm: Modern Dog

Title: Dogs We Know Bag

Art director: Mitch Nash

Designer, illustrator: Robert Zwiebel

Size: 14 × 13.25 inches
(35.6 × 33.7 cm)

Materials: Digital ink, software

Printing process: Offset, printed
on recycled polypropylene

Modern Dog's Robynne Raye explains how showing off the firm's new book of their work to a client paid off with a new project. "Mitch Nash, of Blue Q, saw the pattern we made in the end pages and thought it would make a great bag. All the dogs on one side are ones we know (or know of), and the other side is dogs we don't know—those dogs are made up." The designers didn't want to rely on photography, so the drawings were done using a Wacom tablet.

Firm: Ana Benaroya

Title: Crazy Face

Designer, illustrator: Ana Benaroya

Size: 11 × 14 inches (27.9 × 35.6 cm)

Materials: Acrylic paint

Printing process: Digital print

"I started doing these crazy faces both in my sketchbook and on canvas paper for a purely practical reason," explains Ana Benaroya. "Instead of throwing out the leftover paint on my palette, I began to use it to start an entirely new image. After a while, it would begin to look like a colorful abstract painting. At this point I would revisit my favorite papers and paint over them with these very simple faces. Now it has turned into a weird compulsion of mine and I can't stop," she laughs. "These make for a lot of happy accidents, especially because the background colors are done without any thought and compiled over time. There is something therapeutic about doing these faces. Maybe it's the lack of control in the beginning, or maybe it's the obsessive line-making."

About creating a print for Tiny Showcase, Stephan Britt says, "I started off with a crude pencil sketch, then inked it using an Irish Fancy rat-hair brush and some old India ink I picked up in Bombay—that should give you an idea as to its age. Because I derive great pleasure from wasting time, I then began digitally erasing all the lines I had just inked and started blocking out the basic colors on various layers in Photoshop. After that, I started to hand-paint the assorted elements (sky, trees, disgruntled tortoise, etc.) on bits of scrap paper with tempera, watercolors, acrylics, gouache, oil pastels, crushed berries, and yak butter. I then scanned in each painted piece of the puzzle and reassembled them in Photoshop. This is a technique I've learned to incorporate into my art, due in part to working with wishy-washy art directors and indecisive designers and editors over the years. Like Roger da Vinci always said, 'It's much easier to alter an element or change the color of a painted piece if it's rebuilt in separate layers, as opposed to submitting a flat painting.' This process may take more time (and less talent) than a traditional painting, but it allows greater flexibility for any necessary changes, which can sometimes be faster than having to touch up or repaint an illustration."

Firm: S.Britt

Title: Eddy Went A-Froggin'

Designer, illustrator: S. britt

Size: 9 × 12 inches (22.9 × 30.5 cm)

Materials: Pencil, brush, India ink, paper, tempera, watercolors, acrylics, gouache, oil pastels, berries, yak butter, software, permanent tar heel removal, 8 bars of Fels Naptha, bucket of bleach

Printing process: Archival ink on Hahnemühle printmaking paper

Firm: S.Britt

Title: Rustic Rolf the Troll of Trondheim

Designer, illustrator: S. britt

Size: 9 × 12 inches (22.9 × 30.5 cm)

Materials: Pencil, sketch paper, software, laser printer, Print Gocco PG-Arts, Print Gocco bulbs, B5 screens, Riso inks, paper, Olde English 800, bottle of aspirin

Printing process: Print Gocco on unbleached mulberry printmaking paper

Illustrating an image for Fantagraphics *Beasts!* Book 2, Stephan Britt based his submission around a Norwegian folktale. Doing the drawing ended up being the easy part. "I originally intended a woodcut, but I had to switch over to a Gocco print at the eleventh hour due to the impending deadline," he explains. "I started by scanning the rudimentary, simplistic pencil sketch into Photoshop and then immediately began blocking out the five color layers or separations (yellow moons, green clovers, orange stars, pink hearts, and blue stools). After that, I printed out the black and white separations on a laser-guided printer and burned the screens using Print Gocco's space-age, Easy-Bake lightbulb technology. I then began making the prints using Riso's official Huff-Proof™ ink and following Newton's fourth law of lightest to darkest, joyous to hopeless," he laughs. The final is filled with extra detail. "Of course the digital mock-up was brighter and the lines more crisp, but the Gocco version has more heart, if you can say that a goat-eating troll has heart—and I'd like to think he does," Britt smiles.

BRIDGE ~~OUT~~ OPEN

S.brit

49

Firm: Invisible Creature

Title: Haven

Designers, illustrators: Don Clark, Ryan Clark

Size: Various

Materials: Acrylic, ink, software

Printing process: Giclee

Few firms pride themselves in combining modern technology with past animation techniques like Invisible Creature. When the Clark brothers were asked to do a gallery showing, they enveloped themselves in pop culture artifacts. "Their shop is filled with collectible toys, books, magazines, and furniture," explains the gallery bio. "The unifying theme of these collections is a love for all things midcentury. Contemporary usage of the word *bourgeois* as expletive aside, there's no arguing the average amount of time Americans spend amidst domestic accoutrements. And though the aforementioned clean-lined design motif hasn't quite delivered the optimistic world of its promises, there's still something Zen-like about the sprawling ranch house that fills the American consciousness. The Clarks' pieces are inspired by their love of midcentury architecture and their collectible fetishisms." Don explains the process as "creating everything eventually in vector form. Even the paint swashes that became the shading were ultimately brought into Illustrator. We didn't want to lose the editable nature of the images, not to mention the fact that many of these pieces would be reprinted at over 4 feet (1.2 m) in length. At the gallery event, most people thought the pieces were completely done using traditional techniques (paint and canvas)."

Firm: Invisible Creature

Title: Search the City, *A Fire So Big the Heavens Can See It*

Designer, illustrator: Ryan Clark

Size: 5 × 5 inches (12.7 × 12.7 cm)

Materials: Watercolor, acrylic, ink, software

Printing process: Offset

"When I started conceptualizing for this project, many ideas floated around in my head," explains Ryan Clark. "The album title, *A Fire So Big The Heavens Can See It*, sounded rather intense, but Search the City's sound isn't heavy or aggressive at all. If they had been a heavier band, the job would have been easy—fire concepts are a dime a dozen in that world. But I had to think more creatively. A volcano is the biggest, most intimidating source of fire and heat I can think of. However, given the overall mood of the record, I wanted to convey a peaceful innocence in the cover image, which required a hand-drawn aspect. I had the idea to place this cute little village at the base of this dormant volcano, as if to say the people that lived there assumed if they kindly settled there, the volcano would remain inactive. Stylewise, I think Richard Scarry and Ed Emberley have been embedded into my subconscious from my childhood, and I can see that coming out in pieces like this. I love the kindheartedness of the style—it's like a little world that sees only happy times."

Firm: Invisible Creature

Title: Ivoryline, *There Came a Lion*

Designer, illustrator: Don Clark

Size: 5 × 5 inches (12.7 × 12.7 cm)

Materials: Watercolor, acrylic, ink, software

Printing process: Offset

"My initial concept for the band was an illustrated lion made up of various forms and mediums," explains Don Clark. "At first they were a bit hesitant and weren't too sure of what the final outcome would look like. I supplied them with a few inspirational pieces, and they were gracious enough to eventually give me the green light." Now he had to actually produce this glorious beast. "I placed a photo of a lion on the cover and proceeded to pull out various inks, parts of images, and paint I had created and abstractly chopped them up to create the lion's likeness. I stopped when we felt it actually looked like a lion instead of a mass of color and splatter. I find that whenever I create anything by hand, it tends to be more gratifying. I don't know if it's actually stepping away from the computer or the actual added man-hours in the project, but there is something to be said for bringing an organic element into a project done primarily on a machine."

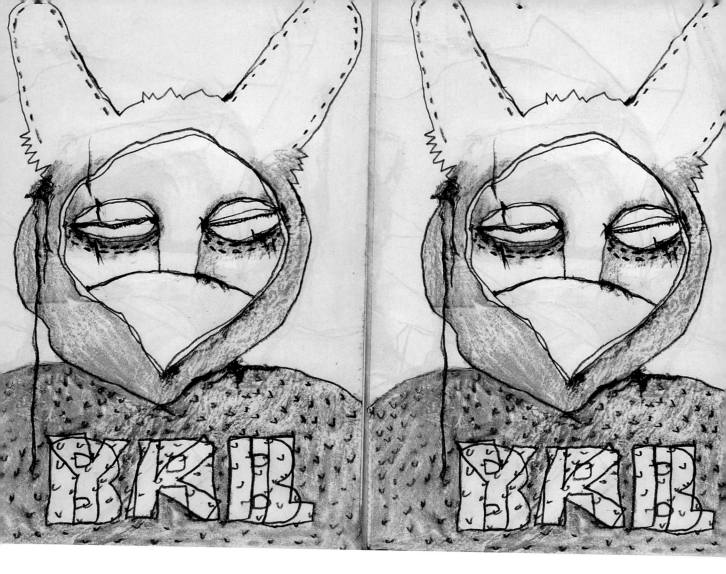

Firm: Jewboy Corporation

Title: Berlin Travel Diary

Designer, illustrator: Jewboy Corporation

Size: 6.75 × 5.5 inches (17.2 × 14 cm)

Materials: Pencils, acrylic paint, ink, photographs, masking tape, strawberry jam, cigarette ashes

Printing process: Handmade

Jewboy says, "I wanted to make a documentary of people, places, and incidents from my journey to Berlin—sort of an illustrated diary." However, he didn't always have his usual tools on hand. "I used materials according to my needs at the moment. For example, I used strawberry jam from a coffee place to color an image red, the ash of a cigarette to make shades around an illustrated house, and so on. It was the only way to document the journey."

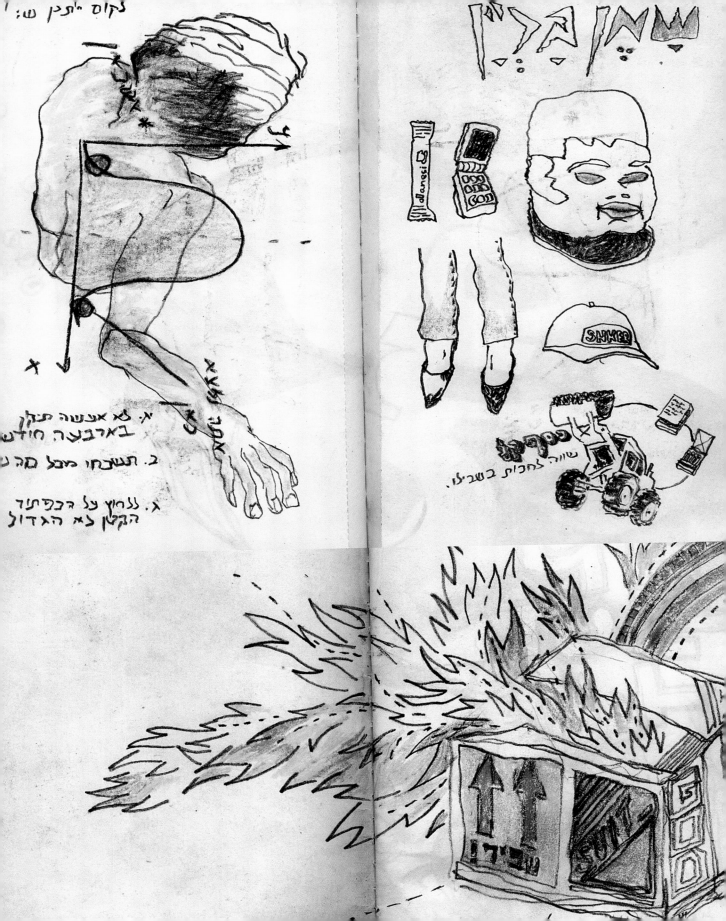

Firm: Mount Pleasant

Title: Melvins/Big Business/Porn

Designer, illustrator: David Bailey

Size: 16.5 × 23.25 inches (41.9 × 59 cm)

Materials: Black pen, ink

Printing process: Screenprinting

"I find the screenprinting process—from original drawing to realization of the finished printed piece—drawn out even though it's not, really," smiles David Bailey. "I'm so used to making posters in black and white and reproducing them by copier, which is fast compared to other methods. I get frustrated with the screenprinting process because you're looking at and handling the image so many times before it gets made that you're sick of it soon after. With black and white, you can just make the flyer or poster and then it's gone; it's out of your hands. Screenprints stick around!" Bailey relates how he came up with the concept: "The drawing of the birdman came from sketching ideas, and it seemed to fit. I wanted to use an image of slime somehow in the lettering because the Melvins sound like slime to me."

Firm: Nathaniel Murphy

Title: Sky Blue Sky

Art directors, designers: Jeff Tweedy, Lawrence Azerrad

Illustrator: Nathaniel Murphy

Size: Original sizes: 18 × 24 inches (45.7 × 61 cm) to 8 × 8 inches (20.3 × 20.3 cm)

Materials: Pen, ink

Printing process: Offset

Illustrator Nathaniel Murphy says, "I produced a movie for avant-percussionist Glenn Kotche's solo shows, which kind of led to me doing the booklet images for the iconic band Wilco, which he also plays in. For *Sky Blue Sky*, I was lucky to be able to work to the demos of the album. What I got out of listening to the record was a simple yet refined approach to what they had been doing in the past few years as a band. I wanted to get at the same thing with my drawings for the album." Murphy decided on "a repetition of individual patterns that, when combined, make up larger and hopefully beautiful images. I've been told there is a subtle melancholy to my drawings, and I think that fits with the album as well. Drawing like this turns into a form of meditation for me. After a while, the scratch at the paper and the repetitive motion from the drafting pen puts me in a trance that can keep me working for hours. I would say that is what keeps me drawing like this—it just takes me to another place that's calming and creatively interesting. Time slows down, and the paper seems to hold endless possibilities. I can start on a piece and watch it slowly take shape organically, sometimes in a completely different direction than I had originally conceived."

◀ **Firm:** Mount Pleasant

Title: The Social October flyer

Designer, illustrator: David Bailey

Size: 8.25 × 11.25 inches

(21 × 28.6 cm)

Materials: Pencil, software

Printing process: Offset

For a flyer for local club called The Social, David Bailey says, "I wanted to do a comic strip on the front of the flyer so people could read it and spend some time on it. Because the flyer is for a venue rather than a band, I wanted it to seem like it was on the level of a cool hangout." Bailey needed to add flat color via the computer and found "an interesting textural vibe and varied line with the pencil against the cold, hard blue steel of the Photoshop fill bucket. The humans look more human, perhaps."

▶ **Firm:** Mount Pleasant

Title: The Twilight Sad

Designer, illustrator: David Bailey

Size: 16.5 × 11.75 inches

(41.9 × 29.9 cm)

Materials: Quill and ink

Printing process: Photocopy enlargement

For *The Twilight Sad*, David Bailey says, "I wanted something big and black and eye-catching, and different from my other posters. It seemed to fit the band and the name also. I wanted to do something where the name wasn't the focus of the poster but still leads your eye to it." He went back to work over the initial photocopy, as it's worth it to take the time to make hatch marks in the black areas to add drama. "If there was just a black filled-in element, you'd lose the weight the hand-inked coloring gives it."

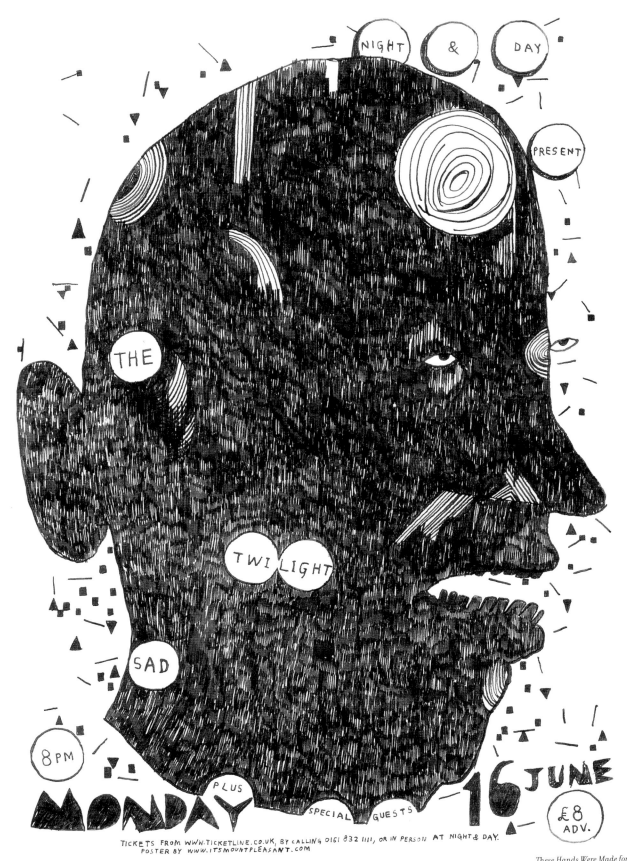

Firm: Mount Pleasant

Title: The Modern poster

Designer, illustrator: David Bailey

Size: 16.5 × 11.75 inches (41.9 × 29.9 cm)

Materials: Pen, ink

Printing process: Photocopy enlargement

"I listened to the band and I guessed the people in their crowd may look like people sitting at the bar," smiles David Bailey. "This poster is part of a series I have done for this venue over a couple of years. The posters always had someone or something sitting at a bar. It was for a venue in Manchester called Night and Day, and the club always makes massive posters to put in their window. I love these sorts of jobs. It's fun to sit down and do the inking in a day and then see the giant results."

Firm: Mount Pleasant

Title: Fanboy

Designer, illustrator: David Bailey

Size: 8.75 × 3 inches (22.2 × 7.6 cm)

Materials: Black ink and acrylic paint

Printing process: Offset on newsprint

David Bailey was hired to draw *Fanboy*, a weekly comic strip that ran on the back page of the iconic British music magazine *NME* from January 2005 to February 2007. "The strips were based on events that were happening at the time—Chris Martin playing on Jay-Z's record, Syd Barrett dying, U2 songs played in church, Lemmy coming out as anti-drugs, and so on. I'd work out the idea of the strip in my sketchbook and then make a rough black and white sketch of how the strip would vaguely look and send it to *NME* for permission to go ahead. Sometimes words were changed, or I'd receive ideas from *NME*. The whole idea-to-finished-strip process would take a day or two, and it was done a week in advance of publication." Bailey loved the handmade approach. "Not many comic strips are hand-painted, but it was the quickest way I could think of to color it, and it looks best that way. It would look lame if I colored it on the computer. I wanted the drawings to stand out and readers to spend time reading the comic, not just do a 10-second scan."

Firm: Mount Pleasant

Title: Ford Maddox Brown

Designer, illustrator: David Bailey

Size: 10.25 × 3.75 inches (26 × 9.5 cm)

Materials: Black and colored inks

Printing process: Digital

"When looking for a classic rock/psych image for Ford Maddox Brown, I returned to a drawing I did in my sketchbook a few weeks earlier," David Bailey explains. "The colors were totally instinctive. I wanted it to look murky. I integrated the text into the image, and I don't know how I would have done that if I didn't handcraft it. It's more exciting for me to work with words and drawings and for each element to influence the others as I work into a piece."

Firm: James Heimer

Title: 19446 Booking Christmas Showcase

Art director: Mike Pelone

Designer, illustrator: James Heimer

Size: 11 × 17 inches (27.9 × 43.2 cm)

Materials: Pencil, pen, India ink, acrylic paint, photocopied pieces

Printing process: Screenprinting

For James Heimer's yearly holiday poster for 19446 Booking, he took advantage of the lack of a headliner and focused instead on "making a comment on consumerism during the holidays." In creating the poster, Heimer says, "I filled all my color separations with graphite on textured paper and then photocopied them, and then I copied the copies until the image was super distressed." Finally, he added more texture.

Firm: Morning Breath, Inc.

Title: Morning Breath, Inc.

(Gallery Work)

Art directors, designers, illustrators:

Doug Cunningham, Jason Noto

Size: Various

Materials: Arylic, enamel, ink, wood

Printing process: Paint and silkscreen

Jason Noto explains, "These pieces are pretty much all inspired by a bygone era. Doug and I were born in the early 1970s, and we often reminisce about the way things used to be. The characters are typical of the burnout type we recall from our youth. The typography is influenced from the peep shows, pawnshops, and places like Times Square in New York and the Tenderloin in San Francisco. It's a reflection of a more down-and-out time, a time before the mass strip-mall takeover, that now makes all of America look and feel the same." That these pieces are "handcrafted from the start makes them interesting, as layers and layers of paint and texture grow in a way you just can't replicate digitally."

Morning Breath, Inc. (Gallery Work) images continued through page 65

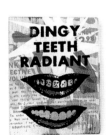

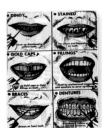

Firm: Morning Breath, Inc.

Title: Sixpack T-shirts

Art directors, designers, illustrators:

Doug Cunningham, Jason Noto

Size: Various

Materials: Ink, software

Printing process: Screenprinting

"The T-shirts we do for Sixpack are completely random," explains Morning Breath's Jason Noto. "We've been fortunate to work with this company that trusts our instincts when it comes to putting it down for them. We have a ton of shit lying around the studio, from old toys and records and books to all kinds of strange foreign packages with incredibly poor printing, that is constant inspiration to what we do. Sometimes we look at things we have in our studio and say, 'Look how badly this is printed. Why would someone do this? This would make such a cool design,'" he laughs.

Firm: Morning Breath, Inc.

Title: *Juxtapoz* poster

Art directors, designers, illustrators:

Doug Cunningham, Jason Noto

Size: 24 × 36 inches

(61 × 91.4 cm)

Materials: Ink, software

Printing process: Screenprinting

On creating a poster for the art and culture magazine *Juxtapoz*, Jason Noto explains, "This piece was inspired by the type of images you would see in something like *The Twilight Zone* or some bizarre 1960s B horror movie. Not over-the-top strange, but just enough to leave you questioning." Noto, along with Doug Cunningham, made the most of a two-color printing process. "We used transparent silkscreen inks to get that third color that occurs when mixing," he explains.

Firm: Morning Breath, Inc.

Title: *Mass Appeal* magazine cover

Art directors, designers, illustrators:

Doug Cunningham, Jason Noto

Size: 8.38 × 10.88 inches

(21.3 × 27.6 cm)

Materials: Ink on Bristol, software

Printing process: Offset

For *Mass Appeal*, the duo at Morning Breath wanted to strip things down for the desired effect. "The inspiration for this really comes from a lo-fi aesthetic, something that might have been found in a punk zine of some sort," explains Jason Noto. "Keeping with a two-color printing process to get that DIY feel, as opposed to the very polished cover you might expect with a hip-hop artist on the cover, was important to us. I think the magazine was a bit skeptical of us wanting to limit the artwork to just black and cyan, but we felt it really gave the look we were trying to achieve. Had this piece been done digitally, it would have felt impersonal."

HOW MANY MUST SUFFER BEFORE THE EXPLOITATION OF WOMEN WORLDWIDE IS STOPPED?

THE QUANTO PROJECT

Firm: Sommese Design

Title: Quanto Project

Designer, illustrator: Lanny Sommese

Size: 18 × 24 inches (45.7 × 61 cm)

Materials: Ink, pencil, tracing paper

Printing process: Screenprinting

"The Quanto Project," says Lanny Sommese, "is a thematic poster competition, held in Milan, Italy, soliciting designs that focused on the increasing problem of exploitation of women worldwide. The silhouetted positive/negative image depicts a female trapped in the coils of a huge snake, which is intended to metaphorically represent 'woman's' exploitation by human slave traders. Obviously, the pink represents the female, and black ink was chosen to heighten the vile nature of her attacker. To capture the 'horrific' theme of the project, I created an image from the result of combining a number of iterations of the pencil drawing I had done on tracing paper. Once the final form was in place, I inked it in to create the silhouetted image you see."

Firm: The Little Friends of Printmaking

Title: 100-Handed Giant

Art director: Jacob Covey

Designers, illustrators: The Little Friends of Printmaking

Size: 7 × 7 inches (17.8 × 17.8 cm)

Materials: Spray paint, grease pencil, India ink, toothbrush

Printing process: Stochastic printing

"This was made for the first edition of *Beasts!*, a modern bestiary. The mythical beasts were allocated on a first-come, first-served basis, so we were lucky to get our first choice," says Melissa Buchanan of The Little Friends. "The choice was predicated on the opportunity to draw lots of hands doing stuff. It was pretty crazy to see famous illustrators fighting over pretend animals." The project started simply enough. "We dipped an el cheapo toothbrush into India ink and flicked it onto the paper to create a pattern of fine random droplets. It's a trick I'd seen on the television show *Reading Rainbow* when I was a kid. Somehow, I filed that away and pulled it out 20 years later for use here," explains Buchanan. Once they had the background, they started building in the layers. "Since this was going to be printed on beautiful stock, we felt it would be a waste if we didn't create something detailed and nuanced that took advantage of the process."

Firm: Morgan Guegan

Title: Jus de Peau et Zidane Forever

Designer, illustrator: Morgan Guegan

Size: 16-page book, 11.75 × 16.5 inches
(29.9 × 41.9 cm)

Materials: Colored ink

Printing process: Offset

Through his use of colored pens and "a clumsiness that cannot be controlled, yet gives a much more personal touch," designer Morgan Guegan set out to make a "book that represents a journey through matter." In order to achieve that sense, he used his pen technique to "decay things in a way they normally would not."

Firm: Weathermaker Press

Title: Califone at the Hideout, 2007

Designer, illustrator: Gina Kelly

Size: 18 × 24 inches (45.7 × 61 cm)

Materials: Transparency, rubylith, film-opaquing
ink, ink, transparency medium

Printing process: Screenprinting

"What's important to me about working by hand is that all the messy little components in the piece become much more evident," explains Gina Kelly of her process. "In digital design, things just kind of pop into your universe with an air of perfection, but it's totally contrary to who we are and how we live. I don't relate to images as well if I can't see any injury or struggle in their making. Sometimes a fingerprint in wet ink or a scratch in an otherwise solid area of color can provide a much-needed sign of life in a piece."

AOOLEU NEWSPAPER

Firm: Aooleu

Art directors: Milos Jovanovic, Tom Wilson

Designer: Milos Jovanovic

Photographer: Gin

Illustrators: Maria Guta, Rob Marshal, Dan Perjovschi, Cristi Neagoe, Ciprian Udrescu, Catalin Matei, Carmen C., Carmen Acsinte, Bruni, Bojan Spasic, Alexandra Paunescu, Alexandru Ciubotariu, Ada Musat, Livia Coloji, Linda Barkasz, Kraiman, Julien Britnic and Sorin Green, Jean Lorin Sterian, Iulian Fratila, Gulia, Gologan, Erps, Vlad Nanca, Vlad C., Sorina Vasilescu, Saddo, Roman Tolici, Rekabu, Oilers, Oana Lohan, Neuro, Matei Branea, Maria Popistasu

Size: A3

Materials: Munken paper, ink, pen, collage, software

Printing process: Offset

Inspired by a "chance meeting with Mr. Tommi Musturi and his gorgeous *Kuti* comic newspaper ," Milos Jovanovic set out to do something similar while capturing the talent available around him in Romania. Built around the still-growing post-Communist comic book culture, a collective has grown to fill the pages of Aooleu with hand-produced design and illustration. Some pages are solo projects, while others are produced by a tableful of visual mercenaries trying to outdo each other. The result is a record of the thoughts and emotions of the Romanian creative class captured at the street level with an unfiltered outlook. Jovanovic relates the experience to a low-tech joy, in having "milk straight from the cow," he says with a mischievous smile.

Firm: Guillaume Ninove

Title: It's a Drawing Book

Designer, illustrator: Guillaume Ninove

Size: 7.75 × 11.25 inches (19.7 × 28.6 cm)

Materials: Ink, acrylic

Printing process: Digital

"I am inspired by daily life, my childhood, landscapes, and my travels," notes Guillaume Ninove. Creating a series of drawings made between Budapest, Bratislava, Cluj-Napoca, Bruxelles, and Strasbourg that are mainly based on the architectural structures, Ninove created an image bank book he can use to make models at a later date for a larger project currently titled "From the Ordinary." Ninove says, "I love to fill up on the places I discover. The most important way of working, for me, is recycling found objects into the art, cutting, and gluing. In the end, I am just trying to highlight ordinary beauty in its most simple and basic way."

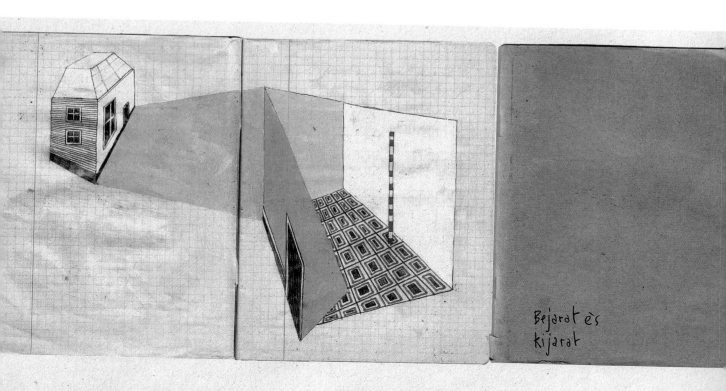

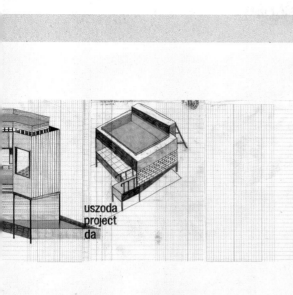

uszoda
project
da

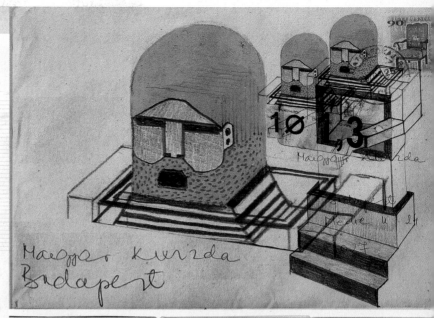

9ø

1ø L,3

Magyar Kurzda

Magyar Kurzda
Budapest

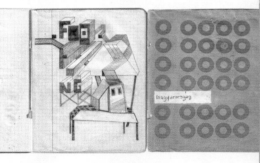

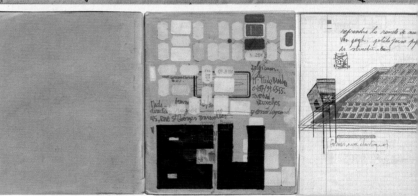

SLOVENSKÝ ROZHLAS

Slovenský Rozhlas
Bratislava (SK)

Firm: El Jefe Design

Title: The Decemberists (series of four)

Art director, designer, illustrator:

Jeffrey Everett

Size: 12.5 × 19 inches

(31.8 × 48.3 cm)

Materials: Pen, ink, software

Printing Process: Screenprinting

"The fun with this project is that people can mix and match the posters to the evenings they would have attended," explains Jeffrey Everett about his series for the Decemberists. "The fact that the shows were over four nights really pushed me to make the posters work on a larger scale as well as promoting the individual nights. I wanted a sense of childlike fun and amusement with the posters, as the band is usually associated with a literary and academic vibe. I took characters from their songs, be it a mermaid or Eli the Barrow Boy, and had them march through the woods. I was very much inspired by old children's books my parents had read to me. The fact that I wanted something cool for my son's room also helped," he smiles.

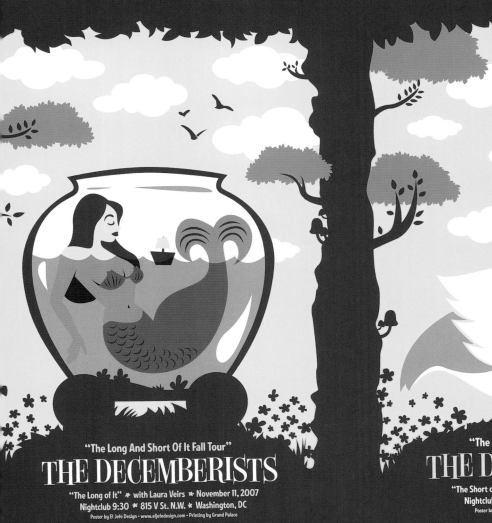

"The Long And Short Of It Fall Tour"

THE DECEMBERISTS

"The Long of It" ★ with Laura Veirs ★ November 11, 2007
Nightclub 9:30 ★ 815 V St. N.W. ★ Washington, DC
Poster by El Jefe Design · www.eljefedesign.com · Printing by Grand Palace

"The Long And Short Of It Fall Tour"

THE DECEMBERISTS

"The Short of It" ★ with Laura Veirs ★ November 12, 2007
Nightclub 9:30 ★ 815 V St. N.W. ★ Washington, DC
Poster by El Jefe Design · www.eljefedesign.com · Printing by Grand Palace

Firm: Yann Legendre

Title: Il Museo

Designer, illustrator: Yann Legendre

Size: 24 × 36 inches (61 × 91.4 cm)

Materials: Pencil, ink, software

Printing process: Screenprinting, offset

"Il Museo in Erba strives to make great works of art accessible to all ages, especially to children," explains Yann Legendre. "I have worked for this museum ever since its doors opened. Not only did I design the logo, I continue to develop the posters for the exhibitions. In each poster I try to create an image that represents or is an allegory of each highlighted artist. At the same time, I want to be sure to develop something that appeals to children. The fabulous director of the museum always lets a group of children decide whether the poster is successful. It certainly is a pleasure to create work that touches children in different parts of the world—in this case, in the Italian region of Switzerland. I put in place a sort of poster system based on the creation of simple and symbolic images in order to allow children to find their own meaning in the art they look at. Little Stories in Art, Citizens of the World, The Magic of Magritte, On a Trip with Gauguin, Leonardo's Coloring Box, and Lautrec and the Moulin Rouge are just some of the playful and educational exhibitions for which I take pride and pleasure in creating the posters and promotional images." Legendre often takes an unusual perspective in associating the artists with their works: "Gauguin and his dog and later refuge, Monet reflected in the water, and even a whimsical sketch for Lautrec—these evoked a sense of curiosity in the viewers rather than offending them."

Il Museo images continued through page 83.

12 febbraio > 16 giugno 04
orari: lu-ve: 8.30 - 11.30 > 13.30 - 16.30
sa e vacanze scolastiche: 14.00 - 17.00
domenica su appuntamento per gruppi.
Festivi chiuso.

il **Museo** in **Erba**
Piazza Magoria 8 / Bellinzona-Svizzera

YANN LEGENDRE

orari : lu-ve : 8.30 - 11.30 > 13.30 - 16.30
sa e vacanze scolastiche : 14.00 - 17.00

domenica su appuntamento
per gruppi. Festivi chiuso.

LAUTREC
et le Moulin Rouge

il Museo iN ERBA
Piazza Magoria 8 / Bellinzona-Svizzera

18 settembre 04 > 19 febbraio 05

in viaggio con Gauguin
7 marzo 09
14 giugno 09

il Museo in Erba

Piazza Magoria 8
Bellinzona
Svizzera

orari: lu-ve:
8.30 - 11.30
13.30 - 16.30

sabato, domenica e
vacanze scolastiche:
14.00 - 17.00
chiuso: festivi

Firm: Bad People Good Things

Title: Sad Crocodile

Designer: John Foster

Size: 18 x 24 inches (45.7 x 61cm)

Materials: Pencil, pen, ink

Printing process: Screenprint

"I went through a phase of animals dominating my illustrations," explains John Foster. For this gig poster, he chose the dapper image of a vegetarian lion. "I create these by working in layers—basically in the reverse manner that the silkscreen is created for press. I paint and draw the original pieces of the illustration but then I work on top of them to create what amounts to be the background so that I can control the ragged overlaps and the knocked out shapes that actually make the body and plate." The final result is a blast of quick energy via paintbrush and pen to create a unique and quirky character to draw you in for the event along with the painted typography.

Firm: Bad People Good Things

Title: Hurricane Poster Project

Designer: John Foster

Size: 18 x 24 inches (45.7 x 61cm)

Materials: Pencil, pen, ink, software

Printing process: Screenprint

"Working with the brilliant people behind the Hurricane Poster Project afforded me a chance to not only assist the victims of Hurricane Katrina, but also to utilize an illustration style I had been working on for years," explains John Foster. Inspired by a comment from his college painting professor to "paint in the graphic way that he designs," Foster had been struggling with that decree ever since. "I knew I wanted the elements to be raw and as primitive as could be, so I drew them in pencil as separate pieces with the smallest number of shapes without connecting anything. Each shape exists on it's own and then they fall in side by side to form the alligators and rooftop and old lady with poodle," he explains. Placed together for the final silkscreen printing, the rawness is apparent and true to the dire subject matter. "The project also made me so proud to actually be able to help as I often feel neutered when something like that happens and my skills don't translate immediately." The final product has also instilled pride in the folks in Louisiana as it hangs in the statehouse.

CHAPTER THREE

WHEN EACH PIECE NEEDS YOUR MAGIC TOUCH

If you are an extremely talented designer, chances are high that you are also an insane control freak. Drawn to a business based on attention to detail and the ability to control a project from inception to delivery of final product can be intoxicating—if not a rollercoaster of worry, most days. In some instances it may be necessary for you, the designer, to take it upon yourself not only to conceptualize and design a piece but also to execute the production and print work. It may be arduous to take on the manufacturing end as well as the design, but it can also be highly rewarding, as seen on the following pages. The result is an imaginative and complete package that allows the design to stand out from the pack. It also satisfies the designer's need to know that not only is every *i* dotted and *t* crossed but also that every last fold and stitch is exactly as desired. This goal is rarely achieved in the normal job flow, which makes it all the more satisfying. Ahhhh…

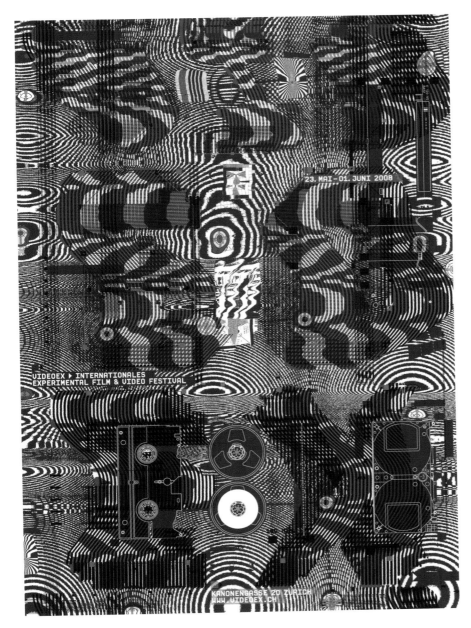

Firm: Martin Woodtli

Title: VideoEx 2008

Art director, designer:
Martin Woodtli

Size: 35.25 × 50 inches
(89.5 × 127 cm)

Materials: Typo, fax pictures,
illustrations

Production techniques:
Fax and screenshots

Printing process: Screenprinting,
four colors

Martin Woodtli draws on his reserve of digital artifacts from video test prints and faxes to assemble the mechanicals for his intricate screenprints. He built layer upon layer of intrigue and complexity into the promotional poster for VideoEx 2008 via this thick mass of roughened digital imagery. Cleverly creating the letterforms by "manipulating your visualization of the test patterns by use of the color" in the printing process, he makes the viewer engage with the piece in unexpected ways as they uncover all of the details.

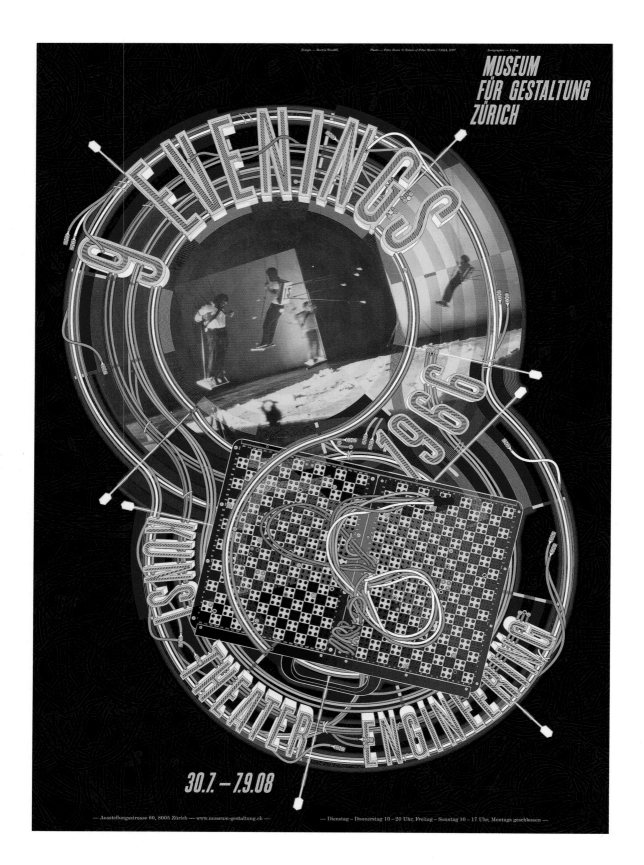

Firm: Hatch Design

Title: Hatch Business Cards

Art directors: Joel Templin, Katie Jain

Designer: Eszter Clark

Size: 2 × 3.5 inches (5.1 × 8.9 cm)

Materials: Egg carton material base, matte sticker

Production techniques: Foil stamping, embossing, hand assembly

Printing process: Offset-printed and engraved with individual names

"Since our firm name is Hatch, it seemed obvious to make our business cards out of egg carton material," says founder Joel Templin. "We tracked down an egg carton manufacturer who let us purchase the flat sheets of the material off the end of a regular order before they were converted to cartons. Probably the most interesting part of the process was that our printer had to iron the sheets by hand in order to get them flat enough to run through the printing press. It took extra effort, but the result was amazing."

Firm: Martin Woodtli

Title: 9 Evenings Reconsidered: Art, Theatre, and Engineering

Art director, designer: Martin Woodtli

Photographer: Peter Moor

Size: 35.25 × 50 inches (89.5 × 127 cm)

Materials: Type, illustrations, photos

Printing process: Screenprinting, five colors

"In 1966, New Yorkers witnessed a series of spectacular events that explored the interaction of artistic performance and technical progress," explains Martin Woodtli. "I designed this poster to promote *9 Evenings Reconsidered: Art, Theatre, and Engineering*, a series of groundbreaking experiments combining diverse genres such as music, theater, dance, film, and video, and put the prominent artists involved—including John Cage, Deborah Hay, Steve Paxton, Robert Rauschenberg, and David Tudor—in contact with experienced engineers. Initiated by Billy Klüver from Bell Telephone Laboratories, it was hoped that this interdisciplinary collaboration would lead to specially designed equipment. It was an historical moment, as the connection between electronics and live performance was being explored for the first time in front of a large audience. This exhibition, organized by MIT's List Visual Arts Center, illustrates the development and implementation of the pieces as well as the mutual curiosity with which art and technology regard one another." The resulting poster takes era-specific neon typography and images of interlocking power supplies showing each element connected to another in intricate detail.

Firm: Hatch Design

Title: Hatch Mobile Self-Promotion

Designer: Eszter Clark

Art directors: Joel Templin, Katie Jain

Copy: Lisa Pemrick

Size: 8 × 11 inches (20.3 × 27.9 cm)

Materials: Egg carton material base, string, software

Production techniques: Debossing and die-cutting

Printing process: Screenprinting

"Hatch Design had just opened its doors, and we needed a promotional piece to announce our taking flight. We had always wanted to do a mobile and we had leftover egg carton sheets from our business cards, so we decided to combine the two things. We used the carton sheets as the base and made the outer wrap with an uncoated French paper stock, the same stock we use for our Hatch stationery and envelopes. The results went beyond our expectations, as the piece ended up on several blogs. To this day we still get requests from around the world to purchase the mobile!" exclaims Joel Templin.

Firm: Hatch Design

Title: Hatch Egg Color Kit

Designer: Eszter Clark

Art directors: Joel Templin, Katie Jain

Copy: Lisa Pemrick

Size: 6 × 7 inches (15.2 × 17.8 cm)

Materials: Wire, crayon, tablets, software

Production techniques: Die-cutting and laser-cutting

Printing process: Six match colors, plus thermography on a spot varnish

"Spring was approaching, and it was time to send out our next promo. Who better to own Easter than Hatch by holding its First Annual Egg Coloring Contest?" says Joel Templin. Hatch wanted to share the fun of creating by hand with those around them. "The custom box we designed contained all the fixings for a perfect egg coloring kit: six magic color tablets, one wire egg dipper, four egg stands, one white crayon, and 50 custom kiss-cut decorative stickers." They added an interactive element to bring everyone together by building out a separate section on their website to host the First Annual Egg Coloring Contest. "The winning entry received a 24-carat gold-plated egg cup trophy. The response was bigger than expected: We sent out only 350 kits but ended up with over 150 entries uploaded to the site, with over 15,000 individual votes being cast. There's also a counter on the site alerting people to the number of days left before next year's competition. Sometimes we really crack ourselves up!" Templin giggles.

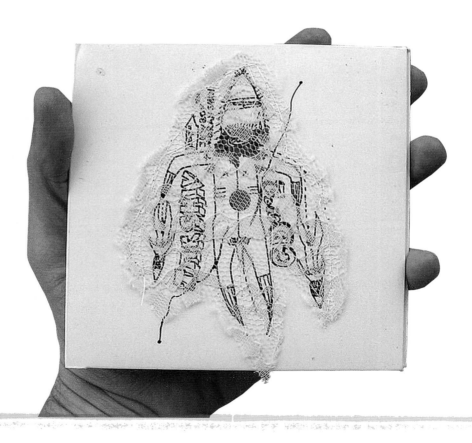

Firm: Jewboy Corporation

Title: TEDER handmade CD covers

Art directors, designers, illustrators:
Jewboy Corporation and Moran Shin

Size: 4 × 4 inches (10.2 × 10.2 cm)

Materials: Carton, illustrations, fabric

Production techniques: Handmade illustration, typography, fabric, lace, thread

Printing process: Handmade

How can you possibly build on the innovative mix of simple innocence and depraved adult situations that collide in the work of Jewboy? By bringing in a collaborator with the same cutting edge sophistication of course! In creating distinctive CD packaging, Jewboy illustrated the initial layouts and then turned them over to fashion designer Moran Shin, who added the fabric detail. "The first edition was experimental, with the intention of making the content 'hidden' as the typography and illustration tried to visualize the general vibe of the music: complicated and fragile, like the combination of the illustration and fabric," Shin explains. Creating the unpredictable, ever-changing covers was hard work, but it has yielded an amazing outcome."

Firm: The Little Friends of Printmaking

Title: Boston Terrier plush + print

Designers, illustrators: The Little Friends of Printmaking

Size: Plush: 5 × 5 inches (12.7 × 12.7 cm); 19 × 25 inches (48.3 × 63.5 cm)

Materials: Needle and thread, twill, felt, poly-fil, cardstock

Printing process: Screenprinting

"For this project, the shape of the plush object more heavily informed the look of the print compared with our earlier forays," says Melissa Buchanan of The Little Friends. "We decided to crop out one area of the print so the two objects would feel more distinct from one another. The original Boston terrier design for the plush form was shaped like a gingerbread man, with arms and legs. We'd originally intended to remove the arms but decided after printing to sew them to the back of the head so the dog's eyes would have that characteristic bulge." Committing to a retail application isn't easy for them, though; "We sewed in a little tag with our logo on it so it would look like a real product . . . well, kind of. For us, it's another way of displaying prints. We're looking for different ways to fill galleries. Maybe we'll make a gallery full of life-size plush print people and then we won't have to go to the opening."

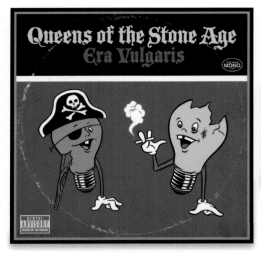

Firm: Morning Breath, Inc.

Title: Queens of the Stone Age, *Era Vulgaris*

Art directors, designers, illustrators:

Doug Cunningham, Jason Noto

Size: Various

Materials: Ink, pen, found art, software

Printing process: Offset

Tongue firmly in cheek, Morning Breath created art for Queens of the Stone Age's record based on sleeve artwork for children's records. "The thought of using mascots to promote products—in this case cigarettes to children—seemed funny to us. We're not really trying to push smoking on kids, but we wanted to push the visual idea of bad for you, or corrupting of young minds," explains Jason Noto. "The color was inspired by a series of old Charlie Brown books from the late 1960s that had a psychedelic color palette." Knowing the look they wanted to achieve, the duo went about making it authentic. "I think the only way to get modern printed works to feel aged, or handcrafted, is to use actual handmade elements," adds Noto.

Queens of the Stone Age, Era Vulgaris images continued through page 97.

BEFORE

ILD THEM UP - *in Min*

OW! **CHARLES OF FIFTH AVEN**

Scandalously brief panties
expertly tailored of sheerest
100% Nylon with contoured
French shadow panel.
Maximum comfort with
minimum coverage   harf et

Firm: Sommese Design

Title: Man and Nature

Designer, illustrator: Lanny Sommese

Size: 18 × 24 inches (45.7 × 61 cm)

Materials: Watercolors, found images, software

Printing process: Giclee

"This image was originally created for a poster I did to commemorate the retirement of one of my colleagues at Penn State, a renowned entomologist who was always bugging me to do posters for his projects," says Lanny Sommese. "Over the years we did a number of projects together. However, because this image was celebrating both my friend's career and man's relationship to nature, I felt an expanded color palette was in order. The image was initially done by hand. The silhouettes of animals, bugs, and so on were produced by tracing images in books. These high-contrast black-on-white (positive) images were then reversed to create white-on-black (negative) versions of the critters. The positive and negative images were then juxtaposed and pasted, by hand, onto a tree image I found in *Silhouettes*, a pictorial archive published by Dover. Once the black-and-white version of the image was finalized I printed out a number of copies, which I colored by hand with watercolors. Because I didn't feel any single version was right, I used scissors to cut out the parts I liked in each and pasted them together to make the final image. I left the cut marks because I felt they added an enigmatic and interesting quality to the visual and added to the humanity of the piece."

Firm: Sommese Design

Title: Hurricane Poster Project

Designer, illustrator: Lanny Sommese

Size: 18 × 24 inches (45.7 × 61 cm)

Materials: Cut paper, found images, software

Printing process: Giclee

"I produced this poster as part of the Hurricane Poster Project," explains Lanny Sommese. "Designers were asked to create posters that related to the devastation caused by Hurricane Katrina. The posters were auctioned off online to help the victims of the horrific storm. My interpretation depicts the victims—humans, animals, and vegetation—trapped tenuously together, each vulnerable to the dangers that surround them." Sommese knew the value working by hand would add. "The fact that the images were cut out by hand imbues the final image with a more self-conscious, human, caring feeling, which adds to the victims' vulnerability and in turn amps up their need for help fast!" His style adds a great deal of power as well. "I frequently employ a technique using the inner contour of one object to define the outer contour of another—a simultaneity of contour. When dealing with shapes rather than lines, the description changes to 'the outside edge of one thing forms the inside edge of something else.' I have developed a style that reflects this type of positive/negative optical interplay between shapes," he explains.

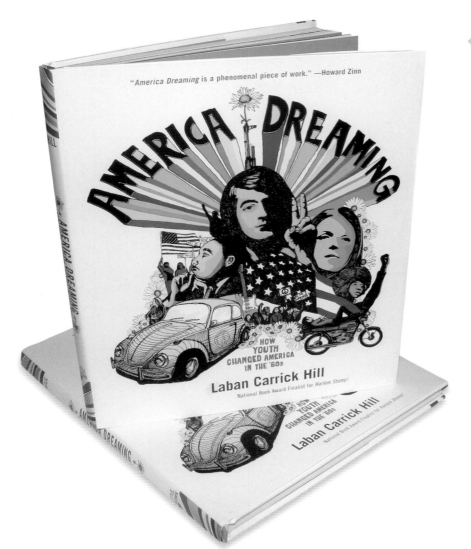

Firm: Modern Dog

Title: America Dreaming

Art director: Gail Doobinin

Designer, illustrator: Robert Zwiebel

Size: 11.25 × 9.75 inches
(28.6 × 24.8 cm)

Materials: Ink, software

Printing process: Offset

"Because the book is about the 1960s and the youth revolution, the artwork had to be authentic," explains Robynne Raye. "The inspiration for Zweibel's illustration came from the Beatles' *Yellow Submarine* movie, but not as cartoony. The result is a more sophisticated Peter Max illustration style." Also, because this is for high school students, "the idea that one is looking at old Pee-Chee art," she says. The image was drawn in ink and then had color applied in the computer.

Firm: Modern Dog

Title: Icograda

Designer, illustrator: Robynne Raye

Size: 18 × 25 inches (45.7 × 63.5 cm)

Materials: Sumi ink, Rubylith, Xerox, X-acto knife, software

Printing process: Screenprinting

Robynne Raye laughs that this poster "was approved, then rejected, then approved at the last minute. In the land of the blind, the one-eyed man is king. The theme of this conference in Seattle was sustainability, and my idea was about the amount of waste generated by disposable consumption that most people don't even think about: plastic cups, lids, and straws. Hence the crappuccino. The message can be interpreted on multiple layers. On the surface we have the coffee-drinking stereotype of the city. If we dig a little deeper we are confronted by the self-indulgent nature of portable consumption and the waste it produces. As a society, we are largely unaware of how a number of corporations operate—they are left to do their job and make money by whatever means necessary. Until people become more informed, these corporations are the one-eyed kings. I believe an enlightened society can create an environment where the most profitable way to operate is also the most responsible."

CRAPPUCCINO

icograda

9-15 July 2006
Icograda Design Week in Seattle

Poster printed on McCoy Silk, thank you Sappi.

Firm: El Jefe Design

Title: Sharon Jones and the Dap Kings

Designer: Jeffrey Everett

Size: 19 × 25 inches (48.3 × 63.5 cm)

Materials: Ink, found art, software

Printing process: Screenprinting

"Sharon Jones and the Dap Kings play music that sounds like it should be coming from car windows in the 1950s," explains Jeff Everett. "This dictated the patterns and color choices. The piece is all about people saying 'I love you' and the consequences of that, whether good or bad. There is nothing as awkward as saying or hearing "I love you" for the first time from a partner. What can the response be? I wanted to portray word balloons as evil little creatures attacking or happy angels comforting the listener." However, Jeff's partner had her own say on the design: "My wife thought it was whale sperm when she first saw the comp. I had to make some drastic edits, which brought about the devil and angel features," he smiles.

Firm: Lovely MPLS / Natalie Schaefer Design

Title: MPLS

Designers: Jamie Paul, Natalie Schaefer

Size: 18 × 24 inches (45.7 × 61 cm)

Materials: Ink, thread

Special production techniques: Each poster is ripped in half and sewn back together.

Printing process: Screenprinting

"The poster was 99 percent thinking and 1 percent sitting at the computer," says Jamie Paul. "Created for an AIGA Minnesota event called 35W Collapse and Recovery, the posters were auctioned off and the proceeds donated to 35W bridge collapse survivors. We wanted a poster that was a simple and elegant solution. The tearing and repairing was the central idea of the concept and was inspired by the question we posed to ourselves: How do you demonstrate the impact of the catastrophic event simply and without literally showing a bridge?"

Firm: Sussner Design Co.

Title: Sussner Design Co. Winter Survival Item #5: The Lunch Spinner

Art director: Derek Sussner

Designer: Brandon Van Liere

Copywriter: Jeff Mueller (Floating Head)

Size: 19.5 × 6.5 inches (49.5 × 16.5 cm); folds into a table tent, 6.5 × 5.5 inches (16.5 × 14 cm)

Materials: Chip board, grommet, cloth mailing bag

Printing process: Offset, screenprinting

"Because we deemed ourselves incapable of coming up with a good luncheon choice—especially on the spur of the moment and while hungry," explains Derek Sussner, "we thought it would be nice to have somebody, or something, make the decision for us. So we designed a lunch spinner for ourselves with all of our favorite local places to eat. With our lunch problems solved and our tummies full, we thought we should share our lunch-location-decider. So we printed 1,000 of them and sent them out to our clients. All in all, we wanted it to be fun and to reflect the personality of SDCo (and our culinary leanings). Trying to come up with enough restaurants to fill a spinner full of choices was fun. With a little inspiration from the attitude of vintage board games we made sure to slip in a few 'go-directly-to-jail' lunch options. What could be worse than actually being forced to eat that cold sammy or can o' soup you brought from home?" he smiles.

Firm: LeDouxville

Title: Secret Stash

Designer, illustrator: Jesse LeDoux

Size: 6 × 6 inches (15.2 × 15.2 cm)

Materials: Ink, score, paper punch, rivets, hammer

Printing process: Silkscreening, letterpress

"The idea of doing this set of prints came after I'd finished one of them with the intention of it being a record cover. However, the concept was quickly rejected by the band," explains Jesse LeDoux. "I decided this single print would work better as a series of four, and as I continued along I knew the series would look best if printed with a letterpress. The idea of it all came together quite fluidly." The process had a greater influence on LeDoux than he originally imagined. "I hadn't shaved for a few days prior to the idea of making the prints. So I decided to make a pact with myself: I'd grow a mustache until the project was finished—an act of solidarity with my little creations," he laughs. "Little did I know the project would end up spanning several months!"

Firm: Axel Peemoeller

Title: Eureka Car Park

Designer, illustrator:
Axel Peemoeller

Size: Various

Materials: Paint, projector,
laser pointer, tape

Printing process: Painting

Simply tasked with providing wall graphics,
Axel Peemoeller insisted on "designing
something that actually interacts with the
user but still makes literal sense. I designed
a way-finding system that works like an optical
illusion as you move around in the car park
space. Once you are positioned in the correct
spot, the letters align perfectly and inform
you which direction to travel in."

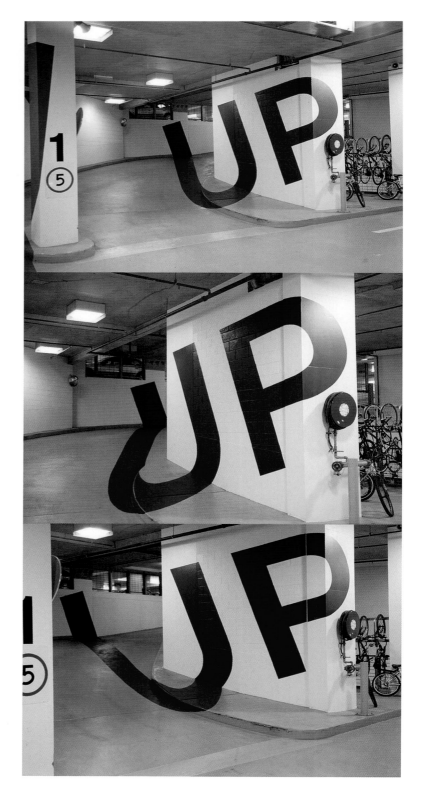

Firm: Axel Peemoeller

Title: Echte Kerle

Designer, illustrator:

Axel Peemoeller

Size: 16.5 × 11.75 inches

(41.9 × 29.9 cm)

Materials: Black gloss tape, knife

Printing process: Offset

Of creating illustrations for *Feld* magazine, designer Axel Peemoeller says, "I filled up on the articles about tough men and their relationship with the sea. I wanted to find a technique that was black and white but gave off this feeling of water and struggle." Creating the illustrations using black gloss tape, he concedes, was an experimental process at best. "You have an idea in your head but you can't be quite sure if it will work as planned, and as you are assembling it the design changes and adjusts with each twist and turn," Peemoeller explains.

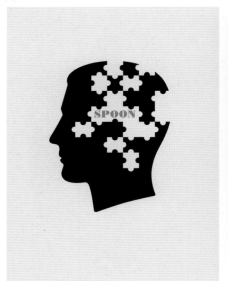

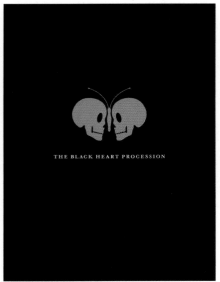

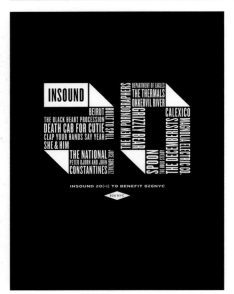

Firm: The Small Stakes

Title: Insound 20

Designer, illustrator: Jason Munn

Size: 18 × 24 inches (45.7 × 61 cm)

Materials: Pen, ink, software

Printing process: Screenprinting

Insound collaborated with Jason Munn of The Small Stakes on the idea of creating 20 images for 20 bands, to be used on apparel and limited-edition posters. "On my end, the bands' music was a large influence, but so was my desire to make all the images work nicely with each other, to make all 20 feel like a set," explains Munn. "I also wanted the images to feel simple and iconic, even on a technical level, because the images had to feel right on a poster as well as shrunk to 3 or 4 inches (7.6 or 10.2 cm) for the front of zip-up sweatshirts." He also wanted them to be special. "The fact that the posters were screenprinted in limited editions added a lot to the overall feel of the project, creating something unique for fans of the bands. Even the shirts were printed in limited numbers," he adds.

Insound 20 images continued through page 113.

the Decemberists

BUILT TO SPILL

CONSTANTINES

CALEXICO

THE THERMALS

JOSÉ GONZÁLEZ

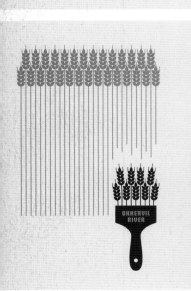

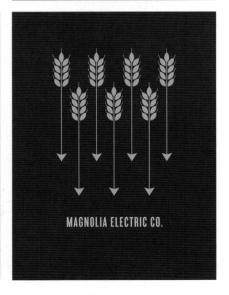

MAGNOLIA ELECTRIC CO.

PETER BJORN and JOHN

DEPARTMENT OF EAGLES

GRIZZLY BEAR

DEATH CAB FOR CUTIE

Firm: HendersonBromsteadArt

Title: 6th and Vine

Art director: Hayes Henderson

Designer, illustrator: Joel Bowers

Size: Various

Materials: Various

Printing process: Various

"I felt like the logo helps convey the laid-back, eclectic feel of the wine bar," explains Hayes Henderson. "It's a little slung together, the same way the bar was. The place is popular because it immediately felt comfortable and lived in, and the logo doesn't get in the way of that aesthetic. Joel created it using some formal but quirky elements like a hand-drawn serif font that seems like an actual font but isn't—it's super simple but not too finished-looking." Once the bar owner had the mark in hand "he did a great job of splashing the logo on almost too many things, but because most are hand-done or one-of-a-kind, it doesn't feel like corporate branding," notes Henderson. "The more he applies it, particularly on unusual elements, the funkier it gets."

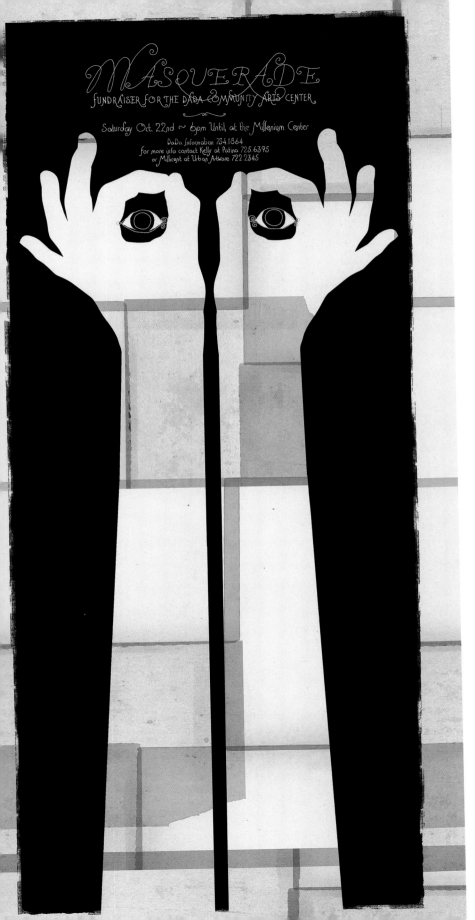

Firm: HendersonBromsteadArt

Title: Downtown Arts District Masquerade Ball

Art director: Hayes Henderson

Designer, illustrator: Will Hackley

Size: 12 × 28 inches (30.5 × 71.1 cm)

Materials: Pencil, pen, yellowed paper

Printing process: Offset

"This event is a bit offbeat and quirky by traditional masquerade ball standards. It's more Mardi Gras than ballroom and cobbled together out of strange pieces and parts," explains Hayes Henderson. "We wanted to do something a little different and referred back to when kids would make hand masks by making loops with the thumb and index finger and mashing it against their face." In order to get the proper feel, the designers needed to do some creating via hand themselves. "The hand-drawn type adds a lightness and tongue-in-cheek faux frilly quality that helps the piece not be taken too seriously. The event was anything but hoity, so the parchment and the hand-drawn type kept it from feeling formal," he adds.

Dining For Friends
Raising funds and awareness for HIV/AIDS
For more information call
275.1654 or visit triadhealthproject.com
June 2, 2007 Dessert finale at
Greensboro Coliseum Special Events Center

Firm: HendersonBromsteadArt

Title: Dining for Friends

Art director: Hayes Henderson

Designers: Will Hackley, Hayes Henderson

Illustrator: Will Hackley

Size: 17 × 32 inches (43.2 × 81.3 cm)

Materials: Pencil, paper

Printing process: Offset

Working with Triad Health Project for well over a decade, the HBA team is "challenged to create an upbeat but not necessarily celebratory image for this yearly AIDS fund-raiser," explains Hayes Henderson. "This concept was so simple that it drove the technique. Why try to embellish something that works in its most elementary state, the sketch?" he asks. However, Henderson adds, "That simplicity is an illusion. We still do a range of sketches that vary in spontaneity to obtain the perfect final image."

Firm: Zach Hobbs

Title: Riverboat Gamblers

Designer, illustrator: Zach Hobbs

Size: 18 × 24 inches (45.7 × 61 cm)

Materials: Ink, Xerox, found art

Printing process: Screenprinting

"Well. The real inspiration for this poster was the thought of the band eating pills. Lots and lots and lots of pills," admits Zach Hobbs. "The second bit of inspiration actually came from a song titled 'Let's Eat,' so conceptually this is pretty straight down the middle. What happens when you have to design a poster for a band that actually has brains? You go for the funny bone. Did I avoid cliché? No way, Jose! The bits of clip art all come from either song themes or stories the band has told in my presence or things I read in zines (yes, they still make those). My favorite part is the little pig running across the middle of the frame." He adds, "The main illustration came from an old encyclopedia, but I jacked it up pretty good, adding the mouth. Layering the colors really brought out something new and fresh. If you can't do pretty, make it ugly as hell."

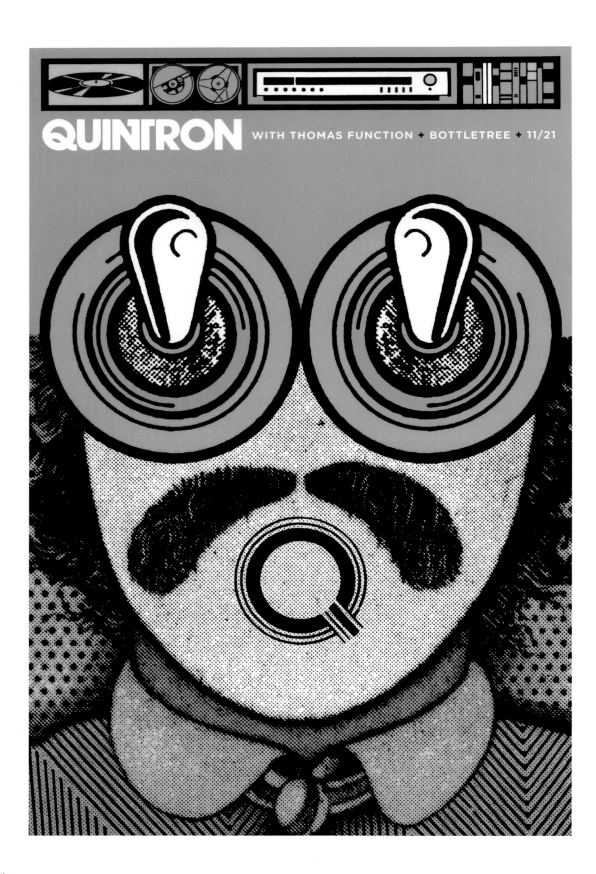

OCTOBER 20 at bottletree
RICHARD BUCKNER
with DAVID DONDERO &
DUQUETTE JOHNSTON

Firm: Zach Hobbs

Title: RCHRD BCKNR

Designer, illustrator: Zach Hobbs

Size: 12 × 18 inches (30.5 × 45.7 cm)

Materials: Ink, Xerox, bamboo brushes

Printing process: Screenprinting

Inspired by "cowboys and campfires. I was poking around on MySpace doing some research into songwriter Richard Buckner and noticed his name was abbreviated as RCHRD BCKNR," explains Zach Hobbs. "I found that really cool, so I couldn't help but use it in the poster. Who needs all those vowels anyway?" He adds, "I was also playing around with some India ink and bamboo brushes and managed to make the really cool flames. You can't go wrong with flames, as long as they look cool."

Firm: Zach Hobbs

Title: Quintron

Designer, illustrator: Zach Hobbs

Size: 12 × 18 inches (30.5 × 45.7 cm)

Materials: Ink, Xerox, type books

Printing process: Screenprinting

"Quintron has a pretty intense live show," explains Zach Hobbs. "Kinda sexual, pretty much 100-percent fun. He is a one-man band, so the idea is machine as man, man as machine. I threw in those cool switches and everything fell into place. I love making faces out of random objects. It's so easy but looks so cool. The switches kind of look like nipples, and the mouth was a 'Quintron as sex superhero.' Really," he laughs. "I really like the little record/reel/stereo image at the top that was yanked from an old magazine. I also find I love patterns and dots. Give me an excuse to use them and I definitely will. You can never have enough dots. Also, this was a process of digging and digging through magazines collecting images and cutting them out as I found them. I constantly collect little things I know I can use one day, sometimes years before they appear. The problem is remembering where I put them."

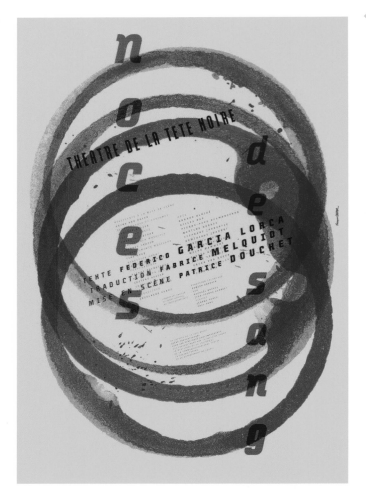

Firm: François Caspar

Title: Blood Wedding

Designer, illustrator: François Caspar

Size: 47.25 × 69.3 inches (120 × 176 cm)

Materials: Ink, glasses, rings

Printing process: Screenprinting

"The famous Federico Garcia Lorca novel *Blood Wedding* takes place in Spain, which inspired the use of the shapes and colors," explains François Caspar. "The hot sun is represented by yellow, and there is a wedding, which brings in the use of rings and glasses as round shapes." He adopts a diabolical smile and adds, "There are murders and wine: red. There are four murders represented by the four rings. The action takes place in one spot; thus, the typography is concentrated inside the ring, like blood drops, fresh and red (new murders) or dried brown blood (old murders)." Caspar needed the emotional quality of working this way because "using handmade shapes, even with tools as objects, like a glass and a ring, let us feel the human being behind the message," he explains.

Firm: François Caspar

Title: Louise/The Bears

Designer, illustrator: François Caspar

Size: 47.25 × 69.3 inches (120 × 176 cm)

Materials: Paint, Sumi ink, water, pencil, brush

Printing process: Screenprinting

"This is a play for children," explains François Caspar. "The story tells us about a girl seeing polar bears and then they melt at the end. Shadows on ice are blue as the ice melts to become water. The proportion between a seven-year-old girl and a polar bear is unbalanced, so for the poster I made the bear's body so big it can't fit into the format. "I wanted to give kids a real drawing with simple elements—a way to educate their eye—to provide a contrast with TV or cartoons. I used a wet sheet of paper to get the dilution of the ink, as the bear is diluted in the end. I made the rough shapes of the nose and the eyes with a dry pencil and a harder brush to balance and get the power of a bear. As I was trying to write the title by hand, my seven-year-old daughter was imitating what I was doing as a game. After a dozen of my poor attempts, I looked over at her work and it was perfect! Children's writing can never be fully mimicked. So I asked her to use her title, and she cosigned the poster, and I took the entire commission," he laughs.

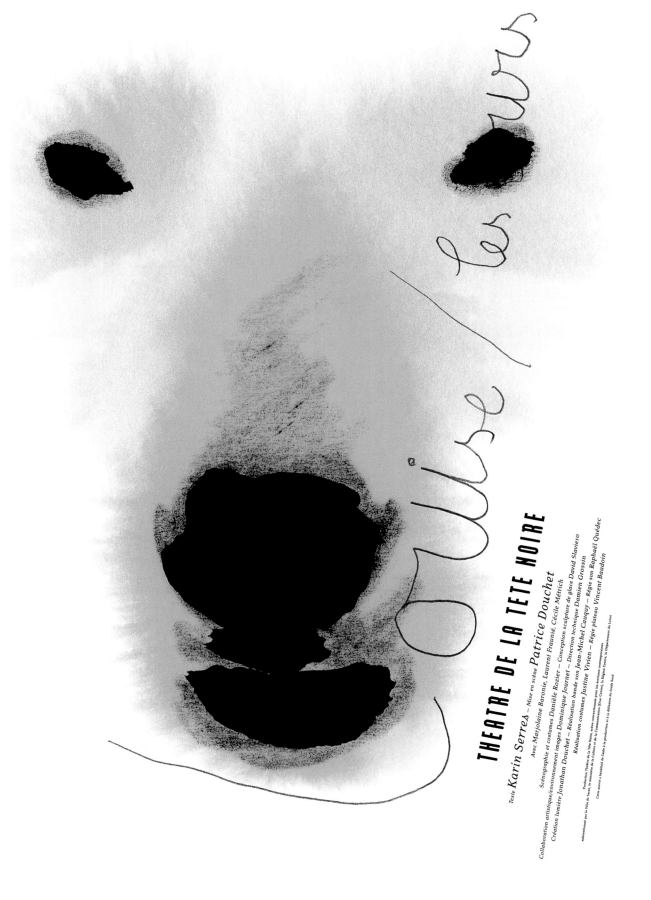

THEATRE DE LA TETE NOIRE

Texte Karin Serres – Mise en scène Patrice Douchet

Avec Marjolaine Baronie, Laurent Fraunié, Cécile Métrich

Scénographie et costumes Danièle Rozier – Conception sculpture de glace David Slaviero

Collaboration artistique/environnement images Dominique Journet – Direction technique Damien Grossin

Création lumière Jonathan Douchet – Réalisation bande son Jean-Michel Cauquy – Régie plateau Vincent Baudoin

Réalisation costumes Justine Vivien – Régie son Raphaël Quédec

Production Théâtre de la Tête Noire, scène conventionnée pour les écritures contemporaines
subventionné par la Ville de Saran, le ministère de la Culture et de la Communication (Drac Centre), la Région Centre, le Département du Loiret
Cette œuvre a bénéficié de l'aide à la production et à la diffusion du fonds Sacd

SASQUATCH! MUSIC FESTIVAL MAY 28, 2005 THE GORGE TICKETS AT TICKETMASTER PRODUCED BY HOUSE OF BLUES SASQUATCHFESTIVAL.COM

Firm: Thinkmule

Title: Ray Lamontagne 1

Designer, illustrator: Jeremy Pruitt

Size: 9 × 19 inches (22.9 × 48.3 cm)

Materials: Pencil, ink

Printing process: Offset

"When I did this drawing, the album Ray Lamontagne was promoting was *Trouble*," explains Jeremy Pruitt. "It had a dancing devil on the cover. I thought it was a great visual, but I wanted my own take on it. I had just visited the Chicago's Field Museum, and they have a wonderful collection of Native American masks. My favorites were from the Northwest region. The concert was also taking place in the Northwest, so I thought it would be appropriate to combine both elements. I think the use of handcrafted art and type lends itself well to Ray's music, and taking inspiration from an ancient culture and applying it to folk music seemed to fit. What is more folk then hand-done type and primitive drawing?" he asks.

Firm: Thinkmule

Title: Ray Lamontagne 2

Art director, designer, illustrator: Jeremy Pruitt

Size: 13 × 22 inches (33 × 55.9 cm)

Materials: Pencil, tea, ink

Printing process: Offset

"Ray really liked the first poster I did and wanted another one in the same vein but different for his next release," explains Jeremy Pruitt. "I went vertical with this one and looked over some more mask artwork to help inspire a new image. Then I combined tea-stained paper and the original pencil drawing to enhance the authentic feel. It is raw, primitive, but the real deal—just like his songs."

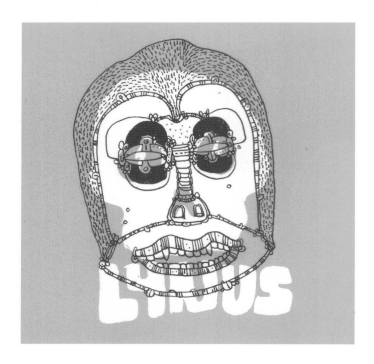

Firm: Thinkmule

Title: Lynus shirt

Designer, illustrator: Jeremy Pruitt

Size: Various

Materials: Pen, ink

Printing process: Screenprinting

"I didn't have music to listen to on this one," laments Jeremy Pruitt. "I just looked at the name and, oddly enough, thought of a gorilla." Once he knew what he wanted to convey, things moved quickly. "I did the drawing with a fountain pen to get some neat line work. I then thought it would be cool to do the skull as a second element. Bam. Done," he says. "I think that hand-done pen and ink is always fun. The lines aren't perfect, and it truly is a one-of-a-kind piece."

Firm: Thinkmule

Title: Stationary Odyssey

Designer, illustrator: Jeremy Pruitt

Size: Various

Materials: Pencil, ink, rough paper

Printing process: Screenprinting

"I told the guys in Stationary Odyssey that I had a drawing
I thought would be great for them," says Jeremy Pruitt.
"I was listening to some of their songs and doodling.
I had just visited a local restaurant that had all these
pronghorn antelope heads on the walls, and I think
it must have sunk into my subconscious and came out
in my drawing. The line work came out great. I did
the drawing with a pencil on a rough paper so the lines
would have a bumpy, un-uniform quality. It held up pretty
well when it was transferred to the screenprinted shirt."

Firm: Thinkmule

Title: Ween, *Shinola* CD

Art directors: Aaron Tanner, Jeremy Pruitt

Designer: Aaron Tanner

Illustrator: Jeremy Pruitt

Size: 5 × 5 inches (12.7 × 12.7 cm)

Materials: Pen, colored pencil, software

Printing process: Offset

Gaining inspiration from the music on the disc, "I got to thinking about what it must be like to be in the mind of the band Ween and all the experiences people have that leads them to create their musical output," explains Jeremy Pruitt. "This led to the cover drawing. I think it needed the rawness of the artwork. The primitive quality of the drawing works well with the music and the band. "The people who follow Ween are pretty hard core, and the artwork had to be true to them."

Firm: Thinkmule

Title: Rent Money Big CD

Art director: Jeremy Pruitt

Designer, Illustrator: Jeremy Pruitt

Size: 5 × 5 inches (12.7 × 12.7 cm)

Materials: Pen, colored pencil, software, marker, spray paint, oil paint

Printing process: Offset

"Rent Money Big is a high-energy band," says Jeremy Pruitt. "They leave it all on the stage every time they play. You always get your money's worth when you see them, and I worked to capture that energy and stage presence. I used a lot of media to build depth in the background, as I wanted the artwork to have an intensity but also a darkness to it. As always, I tried to parallel the artwork with the music. I was trying to make it feel like a bomb is going off, and I think mixing all the different media gave it a lot of energy. All the little parts work together to create a bigger idea where you have ink splatters, pen scribbles, spray paint over spray, paint smudges, pencil scribbles—and then I compiled that into a collage that I think represents the band's music well."

with *nightmare of you* + *colour revolt*

6.29.06 *House of Blues* Lake Buena Vista, FL   **7.1.06** *Ridglea Theater* Fort Worth, TX
7.2.06 *Warehouse Live* Houston, TX   **7.3.06** *La Zona Rosa* Austin, TX

Firm: The New Year

Title: Arma Secreta
with Paper Airplanes

Designer, illustrator: Sasha Barr

Size: 19 × 25 inches
(48.3 × 63.5 cm)

Materials: Ink, software

Printing process: Screenprinting

Knowing the posters would operate
as street promotion as well as
merchandise at the concert, Sasha
Barr wanted to make a statement.
"I really wanted to make a poster
with a space theme and nice type,
but not overdo it," he says. Focused
on a science fiction concept, he
printed on black paper, allowing
the posters to jump off the wall
to the viewers.

Firm: The New Year

Title: Brand New summer tour poster

Designer, illustrator: Sasha Barr

Size: 18 × 24 inches (45.7 × 61 cm)

Materials: Ink, software

Printing process: Screenprinting

To promote Brand New's upcoming summer tour, Sasha Barr's inspiration came from
the band's rabid fan base. "I went with my first idea of critters and just made it work,"
he laughs. The depiction of a flying and hungry little creature mixed in with his vibrant
color selection matches the energy of the band's musical output, as does the poppy-type
execution and the tension-filled bottom half of crisscrossing lines.

CHAPTER FOUR

PUZZLE PIECES

We have touched on the impact of a diverse range of pieces placed in a final image. Here you can see that technique exploited to the fullest. Clean type becomes cutting-edge when juxtaposed with rough, handmade imagery. Found images can be chopped up and placed out of context. Cut paper segments and paint smears mix and mingle with items right out of the box. Spray paint or Xeroxed halftones add visual joy to any piece. Often, it is the single element coming across in such a personal application that provides the greatest visual punch. The amazing quality these designers share is the ability to combine disparate images and elements in a manner that is greater as a whole. Average designers might pair a photograph with some easy type or color blocks. They might fear upstaging the product and not have the guts to grab a paintbrush to create the typography or to manipulate the photo itself. The crafters showcased here know when to pull back and when to push ahead and are constantly organizing elements in their heads. Now it is all on display for you, the precious reader. Enjoy!

THE DELICIOUS FEEL OF SCREEN PRINTING

SWEET

MIXED WITH THE LUSCIOUS TASTE OF INK

FEBRUARY 6 - MARCH 29, 2008 • THE ART GALLERY AT THE UNIVERSITY OF MARYLAND • POSTER BY EL JEFE DESIGN

Firm: El Jefe Design

Title: Sweet: The Graphic Beauty
of the Contemporary Rock Poster

Designer: Jeffrey Everett

Size: 18 × 24 inches (45.7 × 61 cm)

Materials: Ink, found art, software

Printing process: Screenprinting

"I was asked to design a poster for the Sweet exhibition of rock posters at the University of Maryland. The caveat was that the students in the printmaking program would be printing the piece," explains Jeff Everett. "Before starting, I was told no skulls, no bears, no women—it has to be specifically about screenprinting. The limitations made the job easier, actually. The thought of doing a candy bar came from another project I was working on for a chocolatier. Brown and gold are such rich and, um, sweet colors that it seemed natural to make a squeegee and drippy ink, like a melting candy bar." With an exhibit name like "Sweet," it just made sense to add pink. "It took me a while to figure out how to represent the squeegee and ink," Jeff says. "I used photos originally, but it didn't feel right. After many tries on the computer, I stepped back and did a bunch of small sketches where I exaggerated features and made dripping patterns."

COME PLAY WITH US / A CELEBRATION OF THE SHINING / AT THE TIMBERLINE LODGE / TIMBERLINE, OREGON / SHOWING OCTOBER 31, 2008 HALLOWEEN

PRODUCED BY NIKE SPORTSWEAR WWW.NIKESPORTSWEAR.COM / AND FANTASTIC FEST WWW.FANTASTICFEST.COM / AND THE ROLLING ROADSHOW / WWW.ROLLINGROADSHOW.COM

21 & UP / TICKETS AVAILABLE ONLY AT WWW.SHININGPARTY.COM / DESIGN BY JEFF KLEINSMITH / PRINTED BY D.L. SCREENPRINTING

SEPTEMBER 5, 2008 WITH RECORD HOP & MELBA TOAST AT GRANADA THEATER

WAR!

Firm: Patent Pending Design

Title: Mudhoney

Designer, illustrator: Jeff Kleinsmith

Size: 18 × 24 inches (45.7 × 61 cm)

Materials: Old board game, old magazine, software, found type

Printing process: Offset

Inspired by the song "Hard-On for War" by Mudhoney, Jeff Kleinsmith started designing. "I particularly love the message of the lyrics, and the music is some of their heaviest," he notes. In creating a collaged image, he brought the printing process into play. "My original intention was to mix CMYK offset with screenprinting, but the scheduling of the two print processes didn't work out. The addition of the screenprinting would have added a nice accent to the design and a tactile quality, but not having it doesn't compromise the overall design. Using offset changed the way I was able to work, as I was able to use full-color images in the collage." Once he had the image complete, it still seemed to need another touch. "After cutting out the letters by hand I was left with the cut-lines between them, which added a nice warmth. I finished the initial layout and it still had a flat or sterile feel to it, so I created a handmade textured background."

Firm: Patent Pending Design

Title: The Shining

Designer, illustrator: Jeff Kleinsmith

Size: 24 × 36 inches (61 × 91.4 cm)

Materials: Tracing paper, No. 2 pencil, software

Printing process: Screenprinting

Of tackling a poster for the iconic film *The Shining*, designer Jeff Kleinsmith says, "I focused on the film in general, but particularly the scene in the labyrinth when Jack Nicholson is chasing the boy. I didn't want to recreate that scene literally but rather give a feeling of desperation and isolation and madness. I actually sketched the whole thing out before making the poster, which I almost never do. And then I drew the labyrinth by hand before scanning it into my computer to be redrawn more precisely in Illustrator. By doing so, I was able to keep it from getting too clean and precise, which I fought the whole way."

Firm: Jay Vollmar

Title: Volume

Art director: Stuart Alden
(Ink Lounge Gallery)

Designer: Jay Vollmar

Size: 14 × 18 inches (35.6 × 45.7 cm)

Materials: Ink, velvet, software

Printing process: Screenprinting

"When Stuart Alden, the gallery owner, wanted a show called 'Stuff from Jay Vollmar's Basement,' I tried to design a poster that would look like something you would hang in a 1970s-style basement rec room," explains Vollmar. "And because my basement looks like a time capsule from 1974, I designed it to match the tacky décor." Velvet was the key. "This project wouldn't have worked if it was printed with any method other than silkscreen. The tactile nature of a velvet painting wouldn't have come off any other way than by actually printing it on velvet using T-shirt inks." An added benefit of the project was "that a fabric arts studio next to the gallery made pillows out of a few of these," Vollmar adds.

Firm: Patent Pending Design

Title: Cool Hand Luke

Art directors: Jeff Kleinsmith, Rob Jones

Designer, illustrator: Jeff Kleinsmith

Size: 24 × 36 inches (61 × 91.4 cm)

Materials: Cut paper, found images, software

Printing process: Screenprinting

Of *Cool Hand Luke*, "Rob Jones said it better than me, and it's pretty much right on: 'Rich religious symbolism, references, and imagery are deeply embedded within the narrative, with some critics arguing that Luke represents a modern-day, messianic Christ figure who ministers to a group of disciples and refuses to give up under oppression,'" explains designer Jeff Kleinsmith. "The shadowy cross in the middle of the image is representing the Christlike figure, and the lock over the mouth represents oppression, blood for sacrifice. There were a lot of different directions to go with this film, but I was drawn to this idea of Luke as the savior." As engaging as the final results are, they didn't go over well with all. "I got a lot of grief from some of the fans of the movie because it's too obtuse or obscure. I think people wanted a depiction of a classic scene or just Paul Newman's handsome face, but I'm not talented enough to do a scene well or draw Newman accurately. Plus, the client felt it was too exploitive to use his face so soon after his death," he explains. Kleinsmith may not feel confident in drawing famous faces, but his use of cut paper makes this poster sing. "Using hand-cut paper for the cross and prison bars gave the image an unsteadiness I found appealing. I wanted it to have a kind of Polish-film-interpretation vibe," he smiles.

Firm: Jay Vollmar

Title: The Wrens

Designer: Jay Vollmar

Size: 16 × 20 inches
(40.6 × 50.8 cm)

Materials: Ink, software

Printing process: Screenprinting

Sometimes projects come along at just the right time. "I had been working on a series of 3-D pieces, similar to the character on this poster," explains Jay Vollmar. "In the middle of working on one, this Wrens commission came along. Maybe I was stuck in that mode of thinking, but I felt it kind of worked with their music."

Firm: Jay Vollmar

Title: Holy Fuck

Designer: Jay Vollmar

Size: 16 × 20 inches (40.6 × 50.8 cm)

Materials: Ink, software

Printing process: Screenprinting

"I wanted to capture an early 1980s techno look that I felt went well with Holy Fuck's music," says Jay Vollmar. "I needed it to look digital and analog at the same time." The true key to the poster, however, is the inclusion of a pull ticket for a tongue in the musical robot illustration: "The data coming out of the mouth was a separate print that was glued to the back and pulled through a slot cut in the poster," he explains.

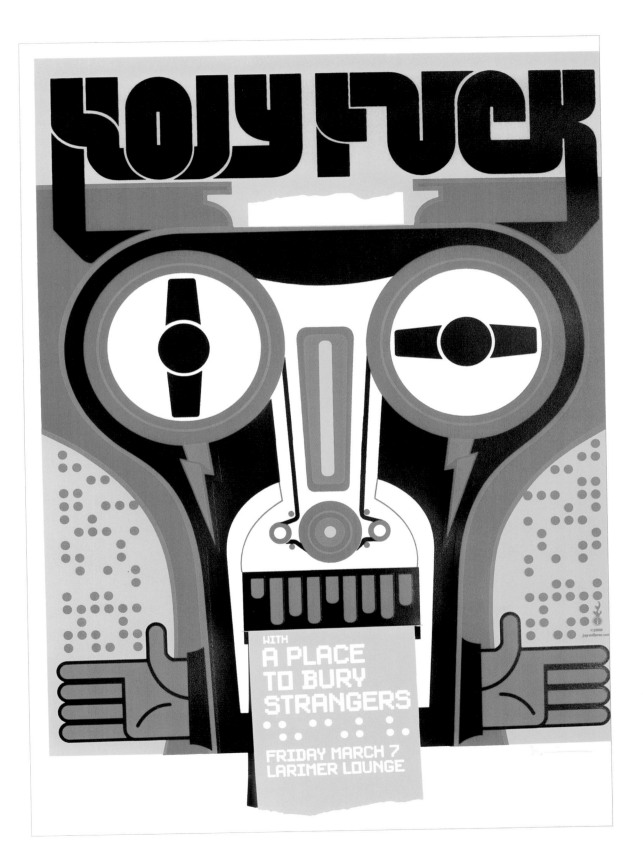

Firm: The Decoder Ring Design Concern

Title: Lucero

Designers: Geoff Peveto and Christian Helms

Size: 20 × 26 inches (50.8 × 66 cm)

Materials: Ink, software

Printing process: Screenprinting

"We often look into the sound and lyrical content of the band's most recent album when starting a poster," explains Christian Helms. "Ben from Lucero always jokes that he's written sixty songs about girls and two about his granddad, so we wanted to focus on his granddad for this one. The visual texture in the piece is a result of mimicking four-color process via screenprinting. After a lot of experimentation, Geoff has gotten really good at this technique, which opens up a broader range of visual solutions."

Firm: The Decoder Ring Design Concern

Title: Built to Spill

Designer, illustrator: Christian Helms

Size: 20 × 26 inches (50.8 × 66 cm)

Materials: Ink, software, Xerox

Printing process: Screenprinting

"One of the hardest challenges can be designing for a band when you don't have any music to reference," notes Christian Helms. "I was stumped because we didn't yet have an advance of the band's new album, so I ended up trying to figure out a visual that was built to spill. A volcano seemed perfect."

SATURDAY, SEPTEMBER 24TH AT LAZONA ROSA ✴ WITH THOSE INCENDIARY INFIDELS THE DECEMBERISTS AND SONS AND DAUGHTERS

POSTER WITH LOVE BY CHRISTIAN@THEDECODERRING.COM

Firm: The Decoder Ring Design Concern

Title: Shout Out Louds

Designer, illustrator: Christian Helms

Size: 22 × 28 inches (55.9 × 71.1 cm)

Materials: Ink, software

Printing process: Screenprinting

"There is a lyric by the Shout Out Louds that goes 'There are things you should keep to yourself,' and I thought I could do something interesting with this," explains Christian Helms. "I wanted to expand the meaning and tell a broader story." He returned to his past concepts from other projects and knew he had found the winner: "The illustration started from a sketch that was nearly the cover of the Modest Mouse album *We Were Dead Before the Ship Even Sank*, which was the perfect starting point for what I wanted to do here."

Firm: The Decoder Ring Design Concern

Title: The Decemberists Origami promotional poster

Designer, illustrator: Christian Helms

Size: 20 × 26 inches (50.8 × 66 cm)

Materials: Ink, paper, software

Special production techniques:

Interns doing origami

Printing process: Screenprinting

"This poster was for the Austin stop on The Decemberist's 2006–2007 tour supporting their critically acclaimed album *The Crane Wife*," explains Christian Helms. "The album is loosely based on the Japanese folktale of a mysterious bride who turns into a crane. What better way to promote it than a poster that does the same?" The designers created a piece that "in just thirty eight short and easy steps turns into a crane!" laughs Helms. Everyone in the office had to suffer a little to bring this to fruition: "Paper cuts. Many, many paper cuts."

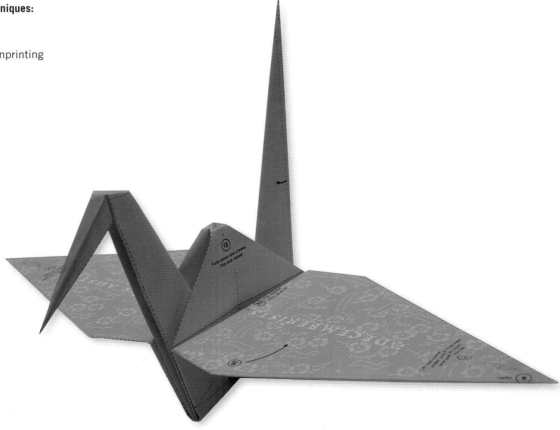

?

DECEMBERISTS CONCERT PROMOTIONAL BOOK

What began as a promotional concert poster project for literary-themed rock band The Decemberists took the form of a book cover for 500 salvaged Reader's Digest compendiums, which were placed in record shops, cafes, bookstores and bars across the city.

Firm: The Decoder Ring Design Concern

Title: Decemberists promo book

Designer: Christian Helms

Size: 22 × 28 inches (55.9 × 71.1 cm)

Materials: Ink, software, old books

Printing process: Offset

"The Decemberists are constantly being described as 'bookish' or 'literary' by the media," explains Christian Helms. The firm figured, why not maximize that to the fullest extent possible? "What began as a promotional concert poster project for a literary-themed rock band took the form of a book cover for 500 salvaged *Reader's Digest* compendiums. Wrapping them with posters, the resulting promo-books were placed in record shops, cafés, bookstores, and bars across the city, creating serious buzz for the event. We ended up with a more tangible object that folks could interact with differently than a poster. Fans brought them to the show, and they fueled interaction between the band and the crowd," he smiles.

"the Good times are Killing me".

VALENTINE'S EVENING WITH MODEST MOUSE AT THE GROVE OF ANAHEIM IN SUNNY CALIFORNIA

THIS IMMACULATE MESS DESIGNED WITH LOVE BY XIAN AT THEDECODERRING.COM

Firm: The Decoder Ring Design Concern

Title: Modest Mouse *Bite the Hand*

Designer, illustrator: Christian Helms

Size: 20 × 26 inches (50.8 × 66 cm)

Materials: Pen, ink

Printing process: Screenprinting

"People connect with work that shows it was created by the human hand. Anything illustrated by hand has an organic quality that tells a story about where it came from and how it came to be. It's a more compelling visual for the audience to interact with," explains Christian Helms as to why he drew the dog in this poster as opposed to finding art elsewhere. Inspired by "the song lyrics and frontman Isaac Brock's relationship with the media—he is not always kind to interviewers who aren't prepared or interested in asking him something new—" Helms depicted a gruesome scene in a playful manner. "Isaac is not a big fan of this poster, but his fiancée loves it," Helms notes.

Firm: The Decoder Ring Design Concern

Title: Modest Mouse "Good Times Are Killing Me"

Designer: Christian Helms

Size: 20 × 26 inches (50.8 × 66 cm)

Materials: lipstick, charcoal, software

Printing process: Screenprinting

"I'm most often inspired by the band's lyrics," says Christian Helms, "and this is a great example of what happens when everything lines up correctly. The goal was to tell a story, using a lyric as a jumping-off point. I had the girl I was dating at the time kiss a white notecard, and I handwrote the display text, and we had ourselves a poster. The extra effort made the difference. Rather than handcrafted, this one was lip-crafted. Had I just illustrated a pair of lips, I don't think the piece would have been as successful. Besides, would you rather spend an afternoon drawing or watching a cute girl kissing things?"

Firm: The Decoder Ring Design Concern

Title: Radical NY AMOA Exhibit Identity and Campaign

Designer, illustrator: Christian Helms

Size: 20 × 26 inches (50.8 × 66 cm)

Materials: Spray chalk, tempera paint, stencil

Printing process: Stencil

"Radical NY is a traveling art exhibition chronicling the rise of the downtown New York art scene from 1974 to 1984. Multimedia works by artists ranging from Haring and Basquiat to Richard Hell and Blondie tell the story of a community that, in ten short years, transformed from a maligned slum to the epicenter of the art world, redefining New York and changing contemporary art forever," explains Christian Helms. "To reference that phenomenon, the logo elevates the lowest form of city life to a level of royalty. The mark was stenciled using nonpermanent tempera paint and spray-chalked around downtown Austin. It was placed (without supporting information) in area newspapers and magazines. In the weeks leading up to the opening, more information was incrementally added to the advertisements until all of the opening information was revealed." The attention to detail was crucial. "You don't want to fake a stencil on the computer," he states, "even if it will eventually be reproduced in a digital format. Crafting the real deal brings the benefit of unexpected textures and other happy accidents that give stencils character."

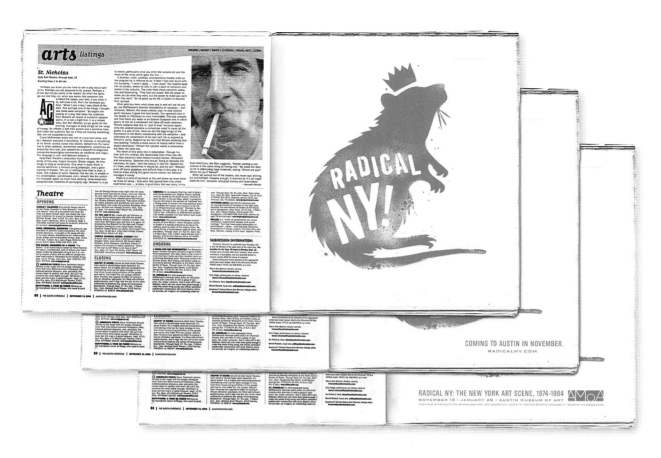

Firm: The Decoder Ring Design Concern

Title: The Hold Steady "Boys and Girls in America" Tour

Designer, illustrator: Christian Helms

Size: 20 × 26 inches (50.8 × 66 cm)

Materials: Ink, software, Xerox

Printing process: Screenprinting

"The whole solution is in the hand-torn element of the poster. Without that, the concept falls apart," states Christian Helms. "The album explores themes of youth, love, and, of course, drug culture. At its center is a line from Jack Kerouac on which the poster is based. Seven hundred sheets were hand-deckled to form the final posters, creating a piece that communicates through a unique marriage of application and material. Building a deckle-form helped make the hand-tearing manageable." He admits, "We really owe our interns for this one."

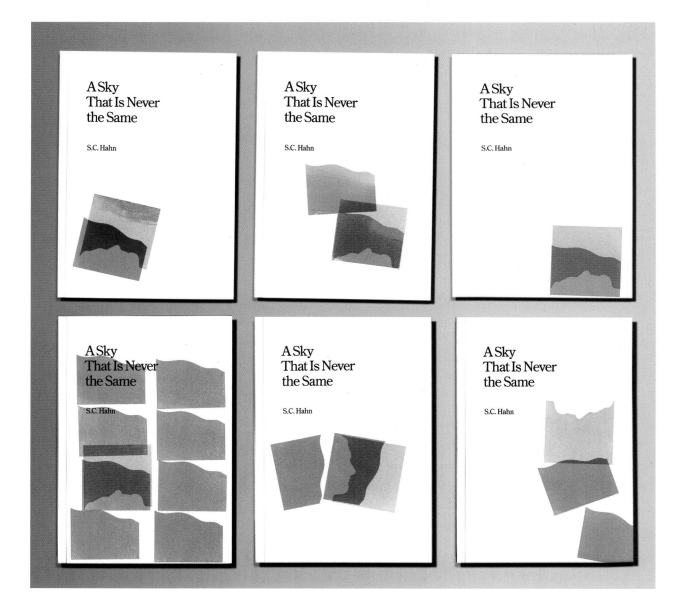

Firm: BankerWessel

Title: A Sky That Is Never the Same

Art director, designer: Ida Wessel

Illustrator: Jonas Banker

Size: 5 × 7 inches (12.7 × 17.8 cm)

Materials: Ink, stamp, software

Printing process: Rubber stamping

"For the cover illustration for a book of poems by Steve Hahn, we made two different stamps—making every cover in a series of two hundred books unique," explains Jonas Banker. "We decided after testing many colors to go with blue and orange because when we printed them on top of each other we got a brownish color we liked. For the cover image we wanted an almost abstract, nature-looking image. The ones we made were of a skyline and the profile of a face, with the face almost becoming a mix between a human and the horizon in nature. Because the poet is from Nebraska, we were aiming for a somewhat American landscape. It took quite a long time printing every cover by hand—almost two days," he laughs. "At first it was quite easy just working with the two colors we decided on, but as the hours went by it was hard staying focused, so I started experimenting with other colors making the images more and more jazz-like. I thought I was making quite funky stuff, but that night I woke up in a cold sweat, certain I had ruined all the books. But when I got to work that morning I was quite happy with the result."

Firm: Sub Pop Records

Title: Flight of the Conchords

Art directors: Jeff Kleinsmith, Dusty Summers

Designer: Jeff Kleinsmith

Illustrator: Tyler Stout

Size: 4.75 × 5.5 inches (12 × 14 cm)

Materials: Pen, ink, software

Special production techniques: Pop-up die-cut

Printing process: Offset

"Originally we had a New Zealand street scene vibe going on until Jemaine from the band mentioned that he liked the craziness of the current Mika record," explains Jeff Kleinsmith. Tyler Stout adds, "Feedback from the band drove this away from a portrait-centered design and more into the art realm, of basically being something cool-looking that reflects the band's sensibilities and style without focusing on pictures of them. Once the cover concept was approved, the rest of the layout evolved from there, carrying the same theme throughout the packaging, which eventually did involve a portrait of Jemaine and Brett." The humor became subtler in the execution as they moved along. Stout's hand-drawn illustrations "took it away from a straight-up nature-inspired scene and more into a Pop Art 1970s style, a surreal landscape of shapes and colors and stuff," he adds.

Firm: Yokoland

Title: The Devil, You + Me

Designer, illustrator: Aslak Gurholt Rønsen

Size: 4.75 × 4.75 inches (12 × 12 cm)

Materials: Collage, software, ink, paint, found materials

Printing process: Offset, matte lamination

"The band was cooperative on this project and let me more or less do whatever I wanted," smiles Aslak Gurholt Rønsen. "The collages made for this cover were created in a different way than my earlier work, as I designed with the bits and pieces almost like I have done before when making paintings." The ability to handle all aspects proved the key, as Yokoland was "able to work on the whole project with a different creative efficiency in combining the images and type and layout and building on or taking away components."

Firm: Yokoland

Title: The Remix Project

Designers, illustrators: Aslak Gurholt Rønsen,

Espen Friberg

Size: 21.75 × 54.75 × 8.75 yards

(20 × 50 × 8 m)

Materials: Cardboard, tape, software

wood pieces, metal

Printing process: Offset, construction

Playing up the aspect of building on a project as a means of remixing it, the team at Yokoland created a promotional poster using collaged elements to push that notion before going a step farther in the actual gallery setting. Constructing letterforms from rough materials and teetering towers of wood bits, they married them with exquisite placement and detail as well as intricate graphics that explode from the wall where the piece leans over and connects.

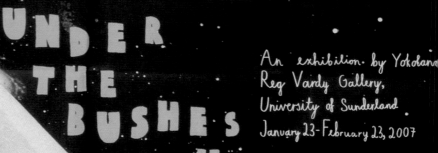

UNDER
THE
BUSHES

An exhibition by Yokoland
Reg Vardy Gallery,
University of Sunderland
January 23-February 23, 2007

UNDER
THE
STARS

Firm: Yokoland

Title: Under the Bushes, Under the Stars

Designers, illustrators: Aslak Gurholt Rønsen,
Thomas Nordby, Espen Friberg

Size: Poster: 19.75 × 27.5 inches (50.2 × 69.9 cm);
wall painting: 54.75 × 1 yard (50 × 3 m)

Materials: Collage, paper, ink, paint, software
wood plates, cardboard

Printing process: Offset, painting

In creating a poster to promote an exhibition of their work, the designers at Yokoland set out to create a collage based around the title *Under The Bushes, Under The Stars*. "Only after the poster and invite had been designed did we transform the gallery space into a huge forest, hanging the work from various plants," explains Aslak Gurholt Rønsen. "We knew we wanted to create an interesting exhibition space that differentiated itself from the traditional white space."

Firm: Yokoland

Title: The Tragedy in the Forest

Designers, illustrators: Aslak Gurholt Rønsen, Thomas Nordby, Espen Friberg

Assisted by: Megan Zolkiewicz

Size: 6.5 × 26.25 × 10 feet (2 × 8 × 3 m)

Materials: Tree, paint, rat

Printing process: Digital

Combining forestry and taxidermy, Yokoland created a playful black and white installation for the Forest Assembly project at the GAD Gallery. Designer Aslak Gurholt Rønsen laughs that the "design concept combines forestry and stupidity." Spinning the common collection of cartoon wilderness characters into an unintended darkness via the demise of the gang's littlest member, the team was happy to acquire a rat with which to work. However, deciding to use an actual tree proved more challenging as the paint buckets awaited. "Drying a freshly cut tree takes much longer than one would expect," Rønsen recalls ruefully.

Firm: Nothing: Something: NY

Title: No Wish to Reminisce (Fargo Records)

Art director, designer, illustrator:

Kevin Landwehr

Photographer: Bill Phelps

Size: 4.75 × 5.5 inches (12 × 14 cm)

Materials: Camera, found objects,

spray adhesive, software

Printing process: Offset

"This album was recorded just as Neal Casal had signed on to join Ryan Adams and the Cardinals. There was an anything-goes creative excitement about him at that time, and the way he put it was that he'd held nothing back, that everything he was as an artist had made it on to this album, and so should we," explains Kevin Landwehr. "The photographer, Bill Phelps, and I pored over the lyrics looking for an emotional core to work from. We conceived of something rich and slightly paranormal juxtaposed with an anachronistic history to add mystery. We began by building tiny sets and dimensional collages filled with object details relevant to the lyrics. Using a Frankenstein camera built entirely from antique parts, we ran three photo shoots: one of still life, one of portraits, and the last of random sparks, flames, and liquids in the darkness. By processing the images in a corrupted homemade chemistry, we created the great little blurs and glitches. Next we applied a light spray adhesive to lightly streaked sheets of poorly exposed Polaroids, fluffed dust and grit onto them, scanned, reversed, and overlaid the color stains and paint textures onto the already moody images."

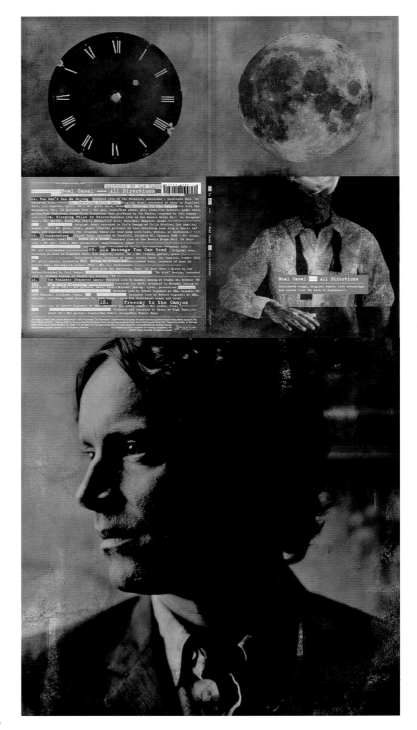

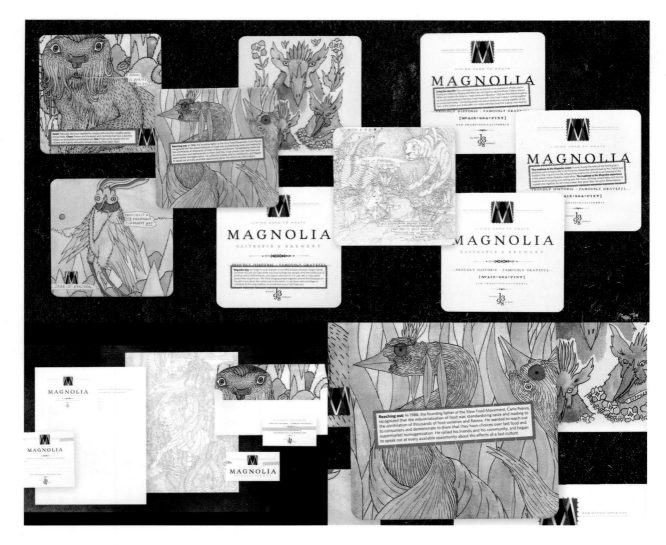

Firm: Nothing: Something: NY

Title: Magnolia Gastropub and Brewery

Art director: Kevin Landwehr

Designers: Kevin Landwehr,
Devin Becker, Melissa Constandse,
Teddy Telles, Tyler Martine, Ray Abeyta,
David McLean

Illustrator: Kevin Hooyman

Size: Various

Materials: Pen, ink, paint, software

Printing process: Offset, foil stamping,
lamination, engraving

"Magnolia Gastropub and Brewery is in the heart of Haight-Ashbury, San Francisco. People come for the food and beer, sure, but they just can't seem to get enough of that 1960s love," explains Kevin Landwehr. "We wanted the work to feel fresh and cool, relating to both the classic Victorian space and the experimental drug culture from the past the area is known for. The logo focuses on a single tab of acid, and everything else follows. For instance, the menus are printed on fully perforated sheets of acid that are then affixed to a book filled with subtly coded Grateful Dead show dates, playlists, bootleg tapings, and historic facts, such as dessert items from the bakery that occupied the space in the 1960s. Intelligently psychedelic illustrations with a modern twist prevent the rich black, silver, and gold tones from creating too moody an atmosphere. There is something noticeably DIY about 1960s-era psych-graphics, but we felt a need to shield more sophisticated customers from the eye-rolling groovy caricature we see as having been commercialized beyond recognition. By integrating the basic warmth and raw, handmade enthusiasm people enjoyed at the time, we could create work people felt comfortable around."

Firm: zitype workshop

Art director: Imagine Wong

Designers: Zheng Huapi,
Li Wei

Illustrator: Zheng Huapi

Size: 16.5 × 22.75 inches
(41.9 × 57.8 cm)

Materials: Pen, ink, photos,
Munken paper

Printing process: Offset,
screenprinting

Imagine Wong says, "I founded zitype workshop to connect design, publishing, exhibition, art, theater, and type research, not just as an overriding philosophy but also in practice." In working with galleries and theaters, he and his team, comprising his fellow Shenzhen University graduates Zheng Huapi and Li Wei, have managed to incorporate such high-minded thinking into economical solutions. In this instance, it is the wonderful drawings from Huapi that combine with the team's sophisticated typography and playful use of real photos (in this case, the heads of the fish for each profile) that make every little detail for *Théâtre sans Animaux* so perfect.

Firm: The Little Friends of Printmaking

Title: Nada Surf

Designers, illustrators: The Little Friends of Printmaking

Size: 19 × 25 inches (48.3 × 63.5 cm)

Materials: Halftone sheets, ink, software

Printing process: Screenprinting

"A lot of our work is concept-driven, but sometimes you just need to make a pretty picture," says Melissa Buchanan about the Nada Surf poster. "We felt it was necessary in this case to do something nuanced and nonspecific in tone and subject. The design was really driven by our technique of using found halftone pieces. Usually we just use little bits and pieces to add texture, but here we've let some of them read as images in order to add flavor to the basic and geometric look of the face. After it was finished, a friend came over and saw it. He said he was drawn to the image because it looked familiar, like a half-remembered dream from childhood, and that it gave him the creeps. It was odd to hear him say that, because he hit the nail right on the head. Without putting it into words, that's what the two of us have been getting at for the past year or two—trying to recreate images that may have never existed in the first place. Mission accomplished!"

Firm: The Little Friends of Printmaking

Title: *Batman* (1966) Movie Poster

Designers, illustrators: The Little Friends of Printmaking

Size: 19 × 25 inches (48.3 × 63.5 cm)

Materials: Halftone sheets, ink, software

Printing process: Screenprinting

"As kiddie TV shows go, *Batman* is absurdly hypersexualized. I don't even need to go into it—everyone knows," says Melissa Buchanan of The Little Friends. "We tried to make a design that would communicate both the innocuous surface messages of Batman and the more sexually suggestive side. Needless to say, kids and adults react very differently to this image." The Little Friends' printing experience allows them to take risks in the production of a piece. "For technical reasons, black is usually the last color laid down in screenprints. This always seemed like a waste to us, as bright colors look so different printed over black. It can be a really interesting effect. So we wanted to create a design where black is somewhere in the middle, with bright colors over the top."

Firm: The Little Friends of Printmaking

Title: Mister God plush + print

Designers, illustrators: The Little Friends
of Printmaking

Size: Plush: 10 × 8 inches (25.4 × 20.3 cm);
print: 19 × 25 inches (48.3 × 63.5 cm)

Materials: Ink, software, thread, twill, felt, poly-fil

Printing process: Screenprinting

Melissa Buchanan, of The Little Friends, admits, "Doing
something complicated such as this—producing a print that
must be cut into a set of specific pattern shapes—is hard.
It required us to do math, which we're not accustomed to.
When you become an adult and get into a highly specialized
field, all that calculus and trig just goes out the window to
make room for arcane design minutiae. While doing this,
we felt at times like cavemen pondering fire or a skull."
The goal of a decent-looking print that could also be
produced as a "soft 3-D object" didn't come easily but
was reached with a brilliant conclusion.

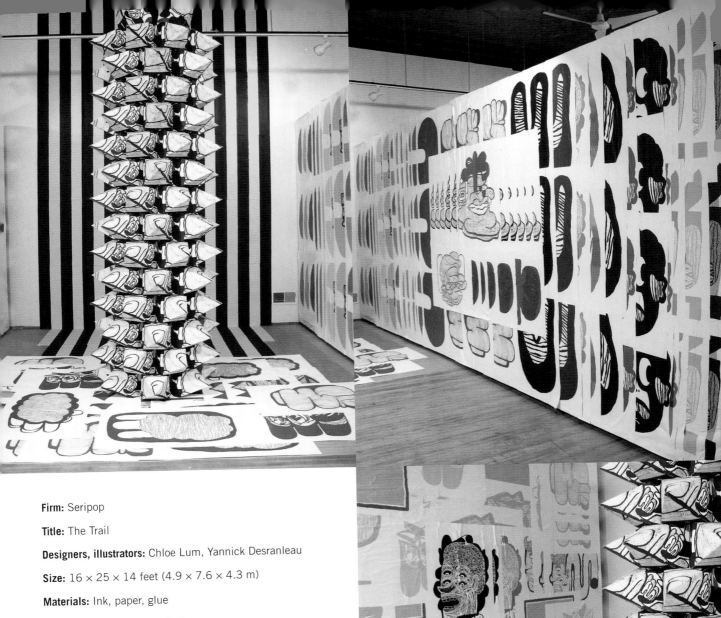

Firm: Seripop

Title: The Trail

Designers, illustrators: Chloe Lum, Yannick Desranleau

Size: 16 × 25 × 14 feet (4.9 × 7.6 × 4.3 m)

Materials: Ink, paper, glue

Printing process: Screenprinting

After years of experimenting with their cutting-edge screenprints, the duo known as Seripop decided to take their two-dimensional work and use it to build three-dimensional installations. "We started experimenting with the direct physical qualities of the prints themselves," explains Yannick Desranleau. "We decided to recontextualize our work and play off the fact that we had been doing virtually a giant street installation with our posters since 2002. This is where we want to see Seripop evolve in the upcoming years—pushing the boundaries of design and combining it with the intellectual research of conceptual art."

Firm: Morning Breath, Inc.

Title: The Lost Ones

Art directors, designers, illustrators:

Doug Cunningham, Jason Noto

Size: 8 × 10 inches (20.3 × 25.4 cm)

Materials: Ink on Bristol, software

Printing process: Offset

Morning Breath used this project as a chance to "let the chips fall where they may," explains Jason Noto. "Using this random approach to designing creates a pattern of happy accidents." The final execution, he explains, was set up as a merging of "1950s/1960s–era comic books and the test prints you would find in a traditional printing press room," with the effect of overprinting the comic figures on the random graphic elements in cyan, magenta, and yellow.

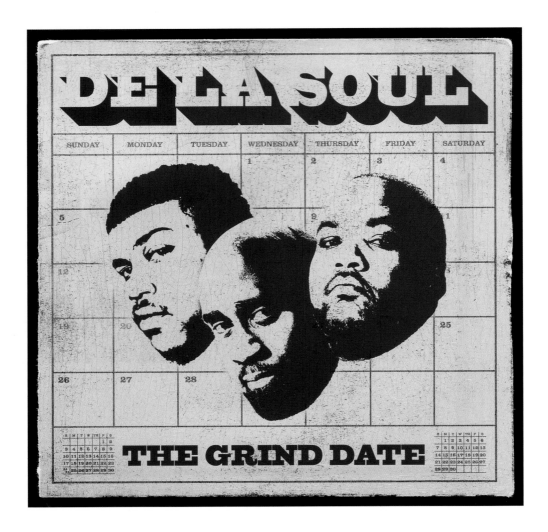

Firm: Morning Breath, Inc.

Title: De La Soul, The Grind Date

Art directors, designers, illustrators:
Doug Cunningham, Jason Noto

Size: Various

Production techniques: Die-cut hole
for hanging calendar

Materials: Pen, Ink, Xerox, software

Printing process: Offset

Using hand-crafted imagery and illustration was critical for Morning Breath's packaging for De La Soul. "The panel art was really inspired by the visual language of early hip-hop and poster art. Many of the panels for the package were designed to look like old-school party flyers," explains Jason Noto. "We even pulled out the old photocopy machine to achieve the flyer feel." A variety of handmade elements were added to the dates. "This was designed as a functioning calendar filled with the group's tour dates, band events, and random appointments."

Photo: Mark Hooper

Firm: Sandstrom Design

Title: Minott's Special Brew

Illustrator, designer: Steve Sandstrom

Size: 12 ounces (355 mL)

Materials: Markers, graphite, newsprint, bottles

Production techniques: Hand-cut and pasted artwork, hand-lettering, hand-aging

Printing process: Photocopy

Not every packaging design project is for a retail product: "I was asked by the creative team of Larry Frey and Stacy Wall of Wieden+Kennedy to help create the make-believe history of Black Star Beer, a new product launch they were handling. We were tasked with elaborately producing packaging to appear as if the beer brand had been around for 100 years," explains Steve Sandstrom. "We made dozens of historical artifacts, and included in the mix was packaging from pre-Prohibition up to the 1960s. The samples shown were created using actual antique glass bottles circa 1860 to 1910. For the earliest brand labels, we created the name Minott's Special Brew as a predecessor to the Black Star brand to add to the detailed depth and realism of the campaign."

Firm: Sandstrom Design

Title: Tazo Tea Shaman's Box

Art director, designer: Steve Sandstrom

Size: 9 × 7 × 1.75 inches (22.9 × 17.8 × 4.4 cm)

Materials: Wooden box, paper, clay, glass test tubes, cork, tin, wax, Chinese coins, flowers, herbs, roots, tea leaves

Production techniques: Produced and assembled by hand; menu cards printed by letterpress

Printing process: Photocopier, Chinese soapstone stamp, letterpress, offset lithography

It can be wonderful when a firm has a client as observant and inquisitive as Tazo. "Our client, Steve Smith of Tazo, found an old wooden science case in the basement of a house he had recently purchased," explains Steve Sandstrom. "The box housed the skeleton of a cat that had clearly been used for biological study long ago. He thought the compartments and old scientific lab style of the box could be reinterpreted as some kind of tea master's kit of ingredients." Sandstrom's team created several boxes with slightly varied contents made up mostly of teas, herbs, and flowers. "The boxes eventually found their destiny as strangely curious vehicles to deliver an afternoon tea menu at an exclusive hotel," Sandstrom notes.

Firm: Sandstrom Design

Title: Billy Bob Jackson's True Corn Squeezins

Art director, designer: Steve Sandstrom

Size: 750 ml (25.4 oz.)

Materials: Antique wicker whiskey bottle, corncob pipe (altered to become a cork), corn husks, wire, wax, rubber band

Printing process: Photocopy

"The concept for this product originated with Edgar Bronfman Sr., chairman of Seagram's, as a select whiskey whose main ingredient was Number 2 Indiana corn," explains Sandstrom. "He wanted to complement and contrast a Southern good ol' boy spirit with a growing urban interest in high-end, distinctive bourbons. We came up with several unique iterations." Unfortunately, the product did not make it to the shelves. "I didn't meet with Bronfman, but I did present the design directions one-on-one with the president of Seagram's America. This took place a few months before the company was sold off in pieces," Sandstrom laments.

Firm: Ana Benaroya

Title: Nerd

Designer, illustrator: Ana Benaroya

Size: 10 × 13 inches (25.4 × 33 cm)

Materials: Acrylic paint, India ink, notebook paper

Printing process: Digital print

"This piece began quite simply—with a piece of paper and extra palette paint left over from another project. The yellow paint reminded me of No. 2 pencils, which led me to the notebook paper, which in turn led me to the thick-rimmed glasses, and so on and so on," Ana Benaroya explains. "The softness of the paint and the imperfection of the lines gives this nerd a unique character. There is an extra layer of depth here with all the different elements combined—and that makes the image more lovable." These projects really challenge her sense of restraint. "I find the hardest thing about some of these faces is knowing when to stop," she confesses. "It's about knowing when to put a line and when to allow the paint to do its own thing."

CHAPTER FIVE

KICKING IT OLD SCHOOL

Certainly one could argue that designers like Art Chantry still paste up mechanicals based on their comfort with that process, but that would be missing the point. Chantry works in that manner because it yields results not easily achieved on the computer. Working smaller than scale can give a final image a certain look, and cutting into Rubylith gives a shape that would inevitably be cleaned up if executed using the pen tool in a software application. And sometimes the issue is not the design; it may be a love affair with archaic forms of production and printing such as silkscreen and letterpress. These print processes allow designers to showcase the idiosyncrasies that emerge when pieces are printed one by one in a hand-generated process. No two are precisely the same, which flies in the face of technological advances in mass production and which makes each print gloriously unique.

Firm: The New Year

Title: Oh No! pocket wallet

Designers, illustrators: Sasha Barr, Meagan Hall

Size: 2.5 × 4 inches (6.4 × 10.2 cm)

Materials: Cotton broadcloth, hem tape, screen print, thread, sweat

Printing process: Screenprinting

Sasha Barr decided to do something useful with the scrap fabric lying around the studio. Looking at his poor battered electronic devices, he had a breakthrough: Why not make a protective, fashionable case for his iPod? Rounding up the extra bits, he cut them into the appropriate size and gave them some silkscreened love. The main challenge (or learning experience) was the size they were working in. "This project let us experiment with tiny design and intricate sewing," he notes. It was all for the best as he (and his customers) can now protect their iPods in stylish fashion.

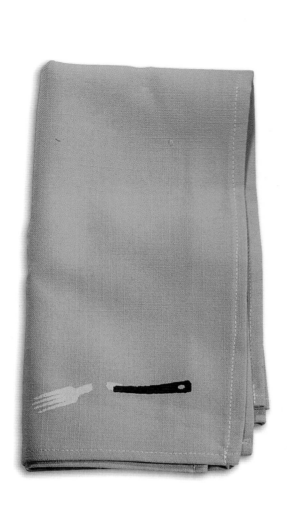

Firm: The New Year

Title: Various placemat and napkin table sets

Designers, illustrators: Sasha Barr
and Meagan Hall

Size: Various

Materials: Cotton blend linen, screenprint,
thread, tears

Printing process: Screenprinting

Sasha Barr and Meagan Hall began making placemats and napkin sets after scribbling on napkins at breakfast. "We used original illustrations and machine-washed and hand-cut materials with screenprinted, machine-sewn, and lovingly folded pieces. It required a lot more ironing than one would think," Barr says. "We started the projects for three reasons: It gives us something to work on during the long winters here in Seattle; it provides the consumer with an option other than throwaway paper products; we took the handmade pledge."

Firm: Scott Campbell

Title: The Warlocks

Designer: Scott Campbell

Size: 12 × 18 inches (30.5 × 45.7 cm)

Materials: Old font book, old children's history book, pen and ink, Letraset spiral pattern, Letraset rub-on letters, software

Printing process: Screenprinting

"The Warlocks' music has a heavy, psychedelic, trance-type feel," explains Scott Campbell. "I wanted to portray that hypnotic quality in this poster." Campbell created the type with letters he scanned from an old font book. The border and the words *Bullhorn Bandits Present* were hand-drawn, and the spiral and other text was laid out with Letraset type and then scanned in. "The figure was taken from a picture of a very old painting I found in a vintage history book." Campbell made the image unique by "blacking out the face of the figure to add an element of mystery and creepiness—and to obscure the identity."

Firm: Scott Campbell

Title: Boris

Designer: Scott Campbell

Size: 12 × 18 inches (30.5 × 45.7 cm)

Materials: Pen and ink, software, roll of decorative bulletin board border, old newspaper

Printing process: Screenprinting

Scott Campbell revealed his resourceful method of working toward establishing a psychedelic and sci-fi theme: "The border elements and crisscrossing lines were drawn by hand, while the unique circular texture in the background was achieved by scanning a roll of decorative bulletin board border on its side. The letters that make up the word *Boris* were scanned from an old magazine advertisement. The main image is an illustration of cancer cells from an old newspaper that I redrew and scanned. The scanner is my friend!" Campbell exclaims. "I redrew it because I'm in love with the rough, natural lines and edges created by putting ink to paper."

BORIS

WITH: **TORCHE & CLOUDS**

TUESDAY JULY 1ST

SPANISH MOON

manplusbuilding

the f#cking cops | you & me got faces | fri jul 25 | spanish moon

Firm: Joanna Wecht Design

Title: Girl Talk

Designer: Joanna Wecht

Size: 16 × 21 inches
(40.6 × 53.3 cm)

Materials: Found images, Xerox, software

Printing process: Screenprinting

Before starting any band posters, designer Joanna Wecht listens intently to the band's music. "I gather several images and I cut and paste little pieces together to make up the main image. I do this for a few hours or even days until something jumps out at me," she explains. "I come up with at least five concepts for every poster I design, but I love it." Wecht works by hand not as much by choice as by necessity. "I do not know how to use computer programs that well. In college I failed Photoshop and had to take it again. I was really bad with the design programs and I had to find a way to get by, so I did everything by hand, cutting and pasting objects and photocopying them, and using found type. I did anything to get by. I still do this," she says.

Firm: Scott Campbell

Title: Man Plus Building

Designer: Scott Campbell

Size: 12 × 18 inches (30.5 × 45.7 cm)

Materials: Old books, software

Printing process: Screenprinting

"Man Plus Building are a relatively new music group and they don't have a lot of pre-existing imagery backing them up, so I wanted to create a poster to help define their identity as crafters of technically proficient, dramatic instrumentals performed with tons of intensity and heart," Campell explains of his literal design interpretation. In the printing, he incorporated "a slightly transparent dark blue printed over the red to create a third color where the overlap occurs." Campbell finds great joy in working this way. "The beautiful grit of the halftone images scanned from old books can't be faked with computer filters."

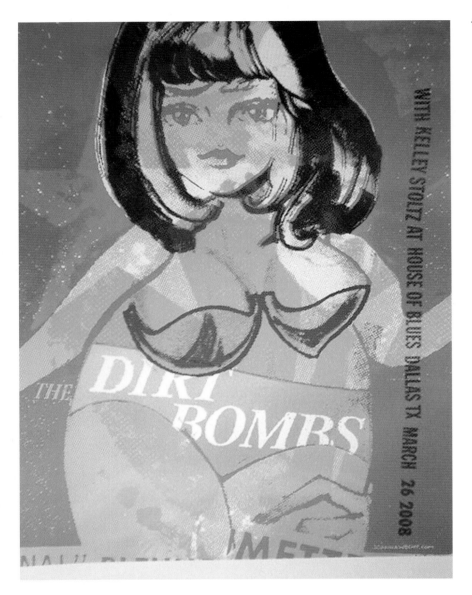

Firm: Joanna Wecht Design

Title: The Dirtbombs

Designer: Joanna Wecht

Size: 16 × 21 inches
(40.6 × 53.3 cm)

Materials: Found images, Xerox

Printing process: Screenprinting

"I seem to always go back to using girls in my posters," says Joanna Wecht. "Once again, I wanted to capture the band's music and give the design an old feel. I looked for images that reflected the band—anything from old car ads or fashion ads—and then I cut them up and put them together. I always seem to leave type last, for some odd reason. To me, the main part is getting the image to reflect the music and the band—then I tackle the type. The type is always from old magazines as well, and it can get tricky to find certain letters, so at times I find myself hand-writing the type."

Firm: Joanna Wecht Design

Title: Black Lips

Designer: Joanna Wecht

Size: 16 × 21 inches
(40.6 × 53.3 cm)

Materials: Found images, ink, Xerox

Printing process: Screenprinting

In capturing the rowdy nature of the garage-punk music of the Black Lips, designer Joanna Wecht says, "I went for the humor side and tried to capture the band's personality—not only in their songs but their live shows. As always, the piece is put together with random images I cut out of old magazines—I put the images together and send them through an old copier. I knew the boobs would be the main element that made it funny," she laughs. "However, drawing them was not easy, so I borrowed illustrator Guy Burwell's perfectly drawn boobs, with permission."

ICE CUBE

WITH MANIAC LOK   FRIDAY, AUGUST 22, 2008
ROSELAND THEATRE   8PM   ALL AGES
PRESENTED BY MIKE THRASHER

Firm: Joanna Wecht Design

Title: Holy Fuck

Designer: Joanna Wecht

Size: 16 × 21 inches
(40.6 × 53.3 cm)

Materials: Found images, Xerox

Printing process: Screenprinting

Designer Joanna Wecht says that when this job came about, "I wanted it to be awesome because I had not made a poster in a while. I tend to overthink a lot of things, and I was really stumped on this one. The deadline was ticking, and I found myself late at night looking for old images I had already amassed. I came up with the female figure and a record player coming out of her head," she notes. "I thought it fit the band perfectly, and it also reflected my style."

Firm: Joanna Wecht Design/Nate Duval Design

Title: Ice Cube

Designers: Joanna Wecht, Nate Duval

Size: 16 × 21 inches (40.6 × 53.3 cm)

Materials: Found images, Xerox

Printing process: Screenprinting

Splitting duties with Nate Duval, designer Joanna Wecht says, "I worked up the main image of the woman's head and then we split up the type. I did the word *Ice* and Nate did *Cube*. He really pulled it together with the colors and the shield on the background." Wecht admits, "It was a challenge for me to do a poster for a rap artist, but I am a fan of all music." The pair worked by emailing pieces back and forth as they slowly built up the final product. "The poster reflects the focus of Ice Cube's music, but it's tasteful enough to grace any wall."

Firm: Ron Liberti

Title: Americans in France

Designer: Ron Liberti

Size: 11 × 17 inches (27.9 × 43.2 cm)

Materials: Found images, X-acto knife, rubber cement, typewriter, Xerox

Printing process: Screenprinting

Taking inspiration from the band's name, designer Ron Liberti says, "I referenced Jean-Luc Godard's classic *Breathless* and combined it with the fact that the band was touring down to the Space Coast of Florida. I thought of actress Jean Seberg taking off like a rocket, just like I imagine the Americans in France are going to do," he smiles. "In the movie, Jean's character is selling the *New York Herald Tribune*, which provided the inspiration for using my trusty old typewriter to create the background."

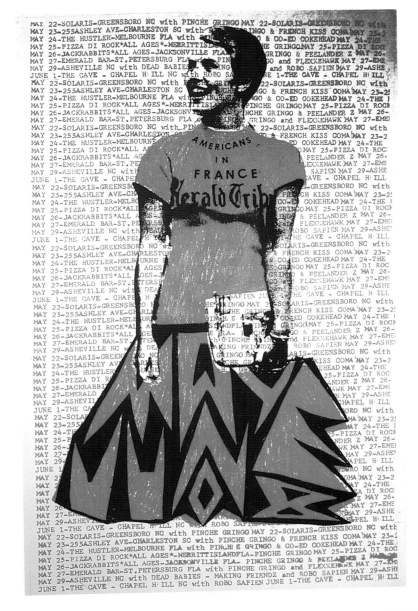

Firm: Ron Liberti

Title: Black Diamond Heavies

Designer: Ron Liberti

Size: 11 × 17 inches (27.9 × 43.2 cm)

Materials: Found images, X-acto knife, rubber cement, pencil, brush, ink, Xerox

Printing process: Screenprinting

"The music of the Black Diamond Heavies conjures up the 1970s, dark and smoky bars, the South, the black velvet paintings of my youth—all of it," exclaims designer Ron Liberti. Working to capture this concept, he began assembling a cool cat figure by slicing and dicing elements and collaging them together, then copying them. He then painted the type in the remaining space.

86

Firm: Ron Liberti

Title: Black Lips

Designer: Ron Liberti

Size: 12 × 12 inches
(30.5 × 30.5 cm)

Materials: Found images,
X-acto knife, rubber cement,
Letraset type, pen, ink, Xerox

Printing process: Screenprinting

Ron Liberti says, "I wanted to make
the poster look like the music,
as I always do. The bands make
music with their hands, and I
wanted to show them the respect
they deserve." For the Black Lips,
he imagines, "If Blacula (the
African-American vampire of
1970s lowbrow cinema) had a band,
it would sound like the Black Lips.
This is a poster for his band.
When he goes home he parties
to Quintron and Miss Pussycat. His
hand is stamped from last night
at the club. He's the real deal."

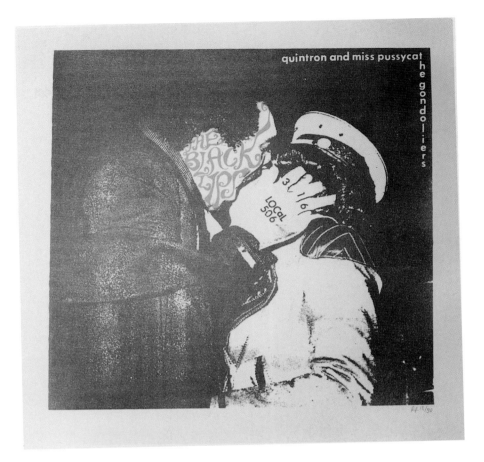

Firm: Ron Liberti

Title: Destroyer

Designer: Ron Liberti

Size: 12 × 18 inches (30.5 × 45.7 cm)

Materials: Found images, X-acto knife,
Letraset type, rubber cement, Xerox

Printing process: Screenprinting

Designer Ron Liberti is a fan of the songs of Dan Bejar, the man behind the band
Destroyer. "It is as if he is writing little movies in every song," he says. Spinning
in a mix of French Canadian culture, voyeurism, and space, Liberti used his
imagination to interpret the artist as only he can. Assembled from various source
material and type books, the images are then photocopied. The final poster
is printed on sheets of paper in different colors.

Firm: Dirty Pictures

Title: Exit Clov Poster

Art director, designer: Anthony Dihle

Size: 12.5 × 23 inches (31.8 × 58.4 cm)

Materials: Found images, ink, camera

Printing Process: Screenprinting

"Exit Clov is about rebellion," explains Anthony Dihle. "Their music is fun. And they're very Washington, D.C, at least in my mind. It is a little bit of an inside joke with locals that the D.C. flag is used as the wick in this petrol bomb. The D.C. flag isn't exactly familiar imagery, but if you get it, you get it. I prepared a Molotov cocktail prop for this poster that I photographed in the windowsill of my living room/print studio. My window overlooks a grocery store parking lot, so I took the photos quickly, lest my neighbors look up at my window and think the worst." He adds, "It feels appropriate that I would print a poster about resistance and homemade weaponry in my home."

Firm: Art Chantry Design Co.

Title: Blood Brothers

Art director, illustrator: Art Chantry

Size: 18 × 24 inches (45.7 × 61 cm)

Materials: Found images, ink, Xerox

Printing process: Screenprinting

"The Blood Brothers name itself, along with their music, sort of sent me in this direction," explains Art Chantry. "I think of them as those kids trying to sound like my generation's music. I know that's unfair, but I feel that way about a great deal of the music being produced today. So, even though I *like* the Blood Brothers' music, I sort of thought of them as little babies simply sucking the blood out of older generations—a true postmodernist appropriation— hence this image. I used an actual baby-doll image from a vintage 1930s toy catalog and a redrawn elongated baby bottle to replicate a long-neck beer bottle. Then I added the label using Cooper Black because it's so retro 1960s nonsense." The baby drinking blood is Chantry's bad attitude coming through. Compiled using photocopier film pieced together and a sheet of Amberlith, he did all of the artwork in about an hour at a cost of under three dollars.

Firm: Dirty Pictures

Title: Hard Tomorrows

Art director, designer: Anthony Dihle

Size: 20 × 12 inches (50.8 × 30.5 cm)

Materials: Found images, ink, camera

Printing process: Screenprinting

"This was the record release concert for two of the bands on the bill. I wanted to feature a disk or record in some way," explains Anthony Dihle. "I photographed a record and a knife and fork, and then I built my mechanical using a transparent black ink to get the same effect as cheaply printed comic books where you can see the colors shift underneath the black ink. You can see where the red ink for the record label stops and the purple ink begins. I think it suggests a severity or rapidity of production. The materials aren't babied; the message is more important than the precision of production. I think that's what I was aiming for, anyway. All the printing in this piece could be sloppy and dirty. Except for the text. This is the smallest text I've ever used for headlining a concert."

Firm: Dirty Pictures

Title: The Shots

Art director, designer: Anthony Dihle

Size: 13 × 23 inches (33 × 58.4 cm)

Materials: Found images, ink, camera

Printing process: Screenprinting

"The Shots' music is dirty and pretty. And I've been looking for an opportunity to use weedy wildflowers like thistles and dandelions. Adding in a good ramshackle vase-like object to hold the flowers was needed. Artillery shell? Nah. Something more improvised and trashy and humdrum—hence the half-gallon milk jug," explains Anthony Dihle. "This is one of the rare cases where I had lots of time to design and print. This piece is twelve colors, plus multiple passes for the red poppies. It took about 10 evenings to print these. When you do it yourself, you can be as lazy or ambitious as you want with the amount of production you bite off. I don't know what a printer would charge for twelve colors, but it feels decadent. For those that printed correctly I think it was worth it."

GREENLAND
WITH
PRABIR & THE
SUBSTITUTES
4.20.08
BLACK CAT
WASHINGTON
DC

Firm: Dirty Pictures

Title: The Shins

Art director, designer: Anthony Dihle

Size: 15 × 23.5 inches (38.1 × 59.7 cm)

Materials: Found images, ink, camera

Printing process: Screenprinting

Overlapping two colors to create a third, Anthony Dihle created something akin to "the music of the Shins—epic and dramatic, but in a quaint, eating-breakfast-in-the-kitchen kind of way. I used a plastic toy boat and rower overlaid with a photo I took of a bowl of Cheerios in my kitchen. The text for this poster I captured from a number of Mexican wrestling posters. I took a lot of digital photos at an exhibit at the Mexican embassy and cut and pasted individual characters from those. There's something satisfying about using a font that isn't really a font, and you know you won't see it elsewhere in town. This was one of about six posters in a row I made involving food. I think there's something inherently funny about food on a rock poster—especially in the context of the desolation or loneliness of one person in a rowboat, and especially if it's an *O*-shaped cereal."

Firm: Dirty Pictures

Title: Greenland/Prabir Poster

Art director, designer: Anthony Dihle

Size: 14.5 × 23 inches (36.8 × 58.4 cm)

Materials: Found images, ink, camera

Printing process: Screenprinting

"This is a pretty straightforward silkscreen piece except that it uses two different screens in two passes, with four different colors to make the kaleidoscope effect in the ice cream bar," explains Anthony Dihle. "The background images are from photos I took of street vendor carts in downtown Washington, D.C. Pictures of ice cream cones, half-smokes, bomb pops. I mixed and remixed inks partway through some of the runs, so colors shift a bit and the black is more solid in some than others. I love transparent black over bright colors. It looks beat, like asphalt. But I had to keep it solid enough to make the text legible. The result is that some prints are warmer in tone than others. Each one comes out differently—like hot dogs on a grill."

all you need is **Love**

John Lennon

stoph8te.org

Rethink Proposition 8

Firm: Modern Dog

Title: Let Leonard In (Sumi)

Designer, illustrator: Shogo Ota

Size: 12 × 18 inches (30.5 × 45.7 cm)

Materials: Spray paint, Sumi ink

Printing process: Screenprinting,

spray painting

"This poster was part of a series intended to drive traffic to the Seattle Aquarium's Leonard website, and posted around in the usual Seattle coffee shops," explains Robynne Raye. "Shogo grew up in Japan, and this poster pays homage to all those years his parents made him take those shuji [Japanese calligraphy] classes." She notes, "The way each sheet was spray painted with red, blue, and yellow before the black screenprint was done can never be reproduced on the computer, and each poster turned out a little different with respect to the way the red, blue, and yellow landed on the paper."

Firm: Modern Dog

Title: All You Need Is Love

Designer, illustrator: Robynne Raye

Size: 18 × 24 inches (45.7 × 61 cm)

Materials: Rubylith, X-acto knife, Sumi ink

Printing process: Screenprinting

"I was asked by my friend Matt Porter to donate a poster to raise funds for stoph8te.org, a website built to raise awareness about Proposition 8, the California ballot proposition that changed the state constitution to restrict the definition of marriage by eliminating the right of same-sex couples to marry," explains Robynne Raye. "I was inspired after hearing Keith Olbermann's televised commentary on his show on MSNBC. I also decided to channel Sister Corita Kent and her all-inclusive message of love. Using the familiar John Lennon quote seemed like a perfect fit to me. The design part was completed in about three hours, even though I spent about three days thinking about what I wanted to do and how best to influence or change people's minds. I talked a lot to friends in same-sex relationships to get a better handle on which direction I went. It was really tempting to just say, 'Fuck! What is wrong with you people?' But in the end, I toned down my assault, and in doing so, I think I was/am persuasive."

Firm: Modern Dog

Title: Hot Shipoopi Nights

Designer, illustrator: Robynne Raye

Size: 18 × 24 inches (45.7 × 61 cm)

Materials: Stencil, spray paint

Printing process: Screenprinting

Using the same techniques they have employed for decades, Modern Dog created a poster for their book release and twenty-first anniversary party at a Seattle club called Nectar. "We had local celebrity Vern Fonk host the evening, and my good friends reunited their college all-girl band, Shit Oven, which played 1980s and 1990s covers. Former student and designer DJ Fourcolor Zach spun records early, while Junichi Tsuneoka created portraits all night. We also had a poster show hung at the club," explains Robynne Raye. "Fun raffle items included Adobe CS3, a K2 snowboard, cupcakes from Cupcake Royale, Modern Dog books and posters, and a Lectro Stik waxer (complete with a supply of wax). My idea was to make it feel like a circus because we had so much going on. It was a super fun night and raised some money for the AIGA, and people loved the poster."

Firm: Ellen Lupton

Title: The Learners: Form/Content

Art director: Nicholas Blechman

Illustrator: Ellen Lupton

Size: 9 × 12 inches (22.9 × 30.5 cm)

Materials: Acrylic, camera

Printing process: Offset

"This piece was made to illustrate a review of Chip Kidd's novel *The Learners* in the *New York Times* book review," explains Ellen Lupton. "I have always been fascinated by the insight once stated by Ferdinand de Saussure, that form and content are inextricably linked, like two sides of a sheet of paper. [Saussure was the founder of modern structural linguistics and semiology.] The review of Chip's novel emphasized the form/content duality, so I chose to illustrate that point. The art knife adds an element of violence (writ small)." To get the proper effect, she printed the words form and content on a sheet of paper and then photographed the paper. "I made a painting of the paper and knife based closely on the photograph; the type was isolated from the original photograph and then dropped on top of a scan of the painting."

"Originally the main bat image was from posters I was putting up around town," explains Andrew McGowan, a.k.a. Kwerty. "I was then asked to submit some work for a show being curated by friends of mine at Moniker Design. The focus of the show was artwork featured on T-shirts and other wearable goods. I decided I wanted to do a tote bag, and I felt just a black bat would be sort of boring and plain. I wanted the bat to have some motion and be colorful, so I put a CMYK streak coming from it. I enjoy projects like this because the majority of my work is done in Adobe Illustrator, and as much as I like working with vectors, everything feels sort of flat and mechanical. So when I screenprint something, it becomes more personal and real."

Designing as a printmaker can produce amazing results when you maximize old machinery. Liisa Graham says, "I printed this poster on a Vandercook 320G composing room cylinder press. This letterpress machine was designed for use in newspaper offices to proof full pages of composed metal type in galleys. The design was made under significant production parameters. At that time, all the large galleys were being used, filled with composed type for other jobs. So, we had to use skinny lino galleys to compose this poster. That explains the poster's design composition." It wasn't just the machinery that informed the design, of course. "Like much of Trip Print Press's early portfolio, the design was inspired by Dutch and Russian constructivist styles and processes," Graham adds.

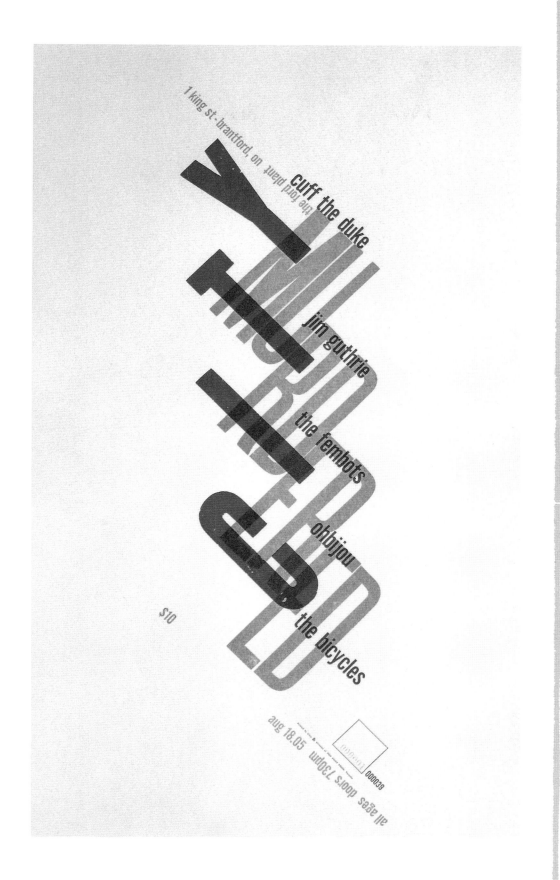

1 king st - brantford, on
the ford plant
cuff the duke
jim guthrie
the fembots
ohbijou
the bicycles
$10
aug 18.05 doors 7:30pm
all ages
650000 100000

Firm: Morgan Guegan

Title: Plastic Age

Designer, illustrator, photographer:

Morgan Guegan

Size: 56-page book, 33.25 × 23.25

inches (84.5 × 59 cm)

Materials: Duct tape, ink

Printing process: Offset

Morgan Guegan says, "I created a book about my views on the relationship man has with his surrounding objects." He chose to physically insert an object in the form of duct tape into his work. "I want the styles and textures to impose themselves and bring the viewer's focus in on the concept and narration." Guegan emerges with a piece where communication overrides the inventive use of a low-tech object.

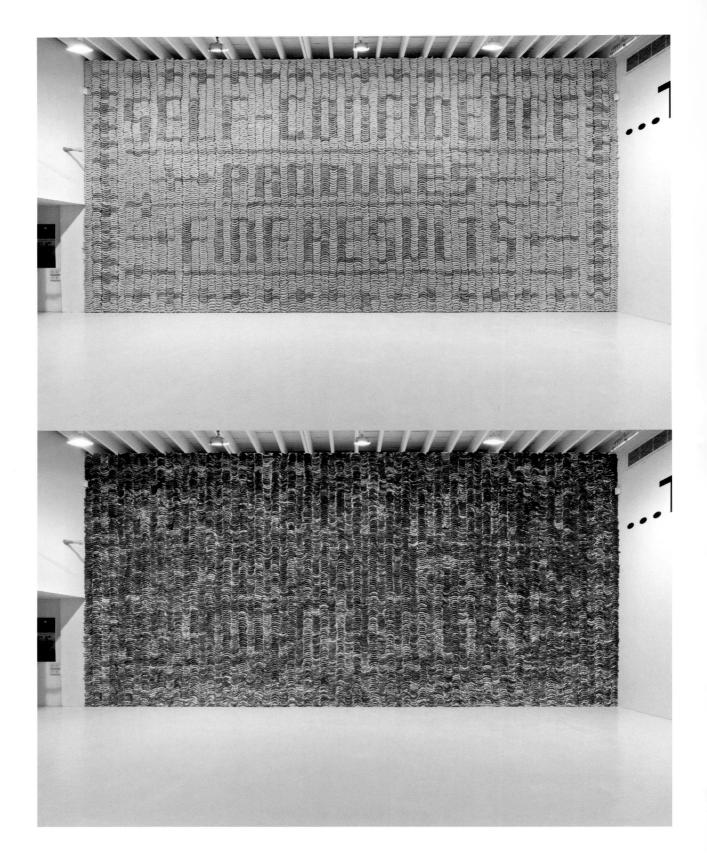

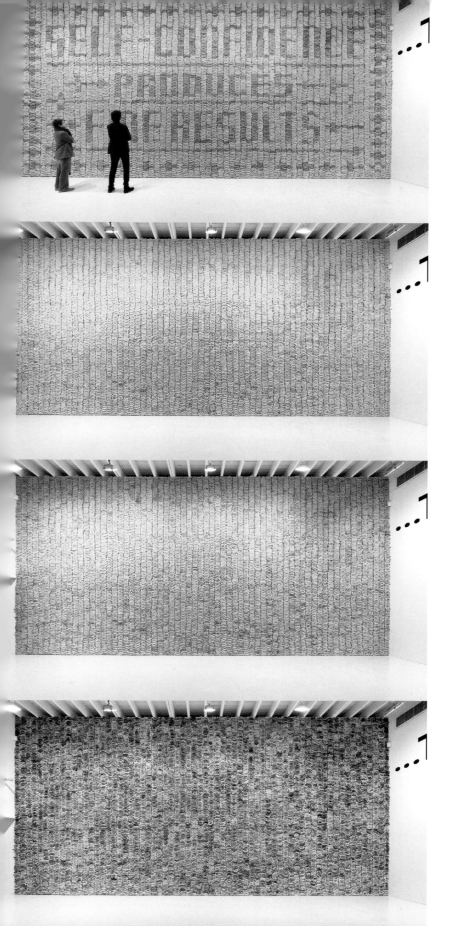

Firm: Sagmeister, Inc.

Title: Banana Wall

Art director: Stefan Sagmeister

Designers: Richard The, Joe Shouldice

Size: 18 × 38 feet (5.5 × 11.6 m)

Materials: Bananas, bananas, and more bananas

Printing process: Installation

Stefan Sagmeister's explorations in created typography were about to take a new turn. "At the opening of our exhibition at Deitch Projects in New York, we featured a wall of 10,000 bananas. Green bananas created a pattern against a background of yellow bananas spelling out the sentiment 'Self-confidence produces fine results.' After a number of days, the green bananas turned yellow and the type disappeared," reports Sagmeister.

Firm: Denny Schmickle Design

Title: Holiday cards

Designer: Denny Schmickle

Size: 4 × 6 inches (10.2 × 15.2 cm)

Materials: Test prints, ink

Printing process: Screenprinting

Denny Schmickle screenprinted his holiday cards onto old posters and test prints he had in his shop, creating a unique holiday greeting for each recipient. "I really love the random, dense, and unpredictable layering of the test prints and the serendipitous new images that emerge when the holiday images are printed on top," he explains. "It makes for an interesting and organic design." The longer you view the cards, the more details emerge. "My favorite part is finding all the old posters and prints that mix together beneath the holiday prints. And I'll always love the gritty, textural surface of a hand-pulled silkscreen," he smiles.

DIRECTORY OF CONTRIBUTORS

AOOLEU
www.aooleu.ro

BANKERWESSEL
www.bankerwessel.com

BAD PEOPLE GOOD THINGS
www.badpeoplegoodthings.com

ANA BENAROYA
www.anabenaroya.com

S.BRITT
www.sbritt.com

SCOTT CAMPBELL
www.scottcampbell.carbonmade.com

FRANCOIS CASPAR
www.françoiscaspar.com

ART CHANTRY DESIGN CO.
www.artchantry.com

THE DECODER RING DESIGN CONCERN
www.thedecoderring.com

DIRTY PICTURES
www.ant-hive.com/dirtypictures

NATE DUVAL DESIGN
www.nateduval.com

EL JEFE DESIGN
www.eljefedesign.com

ODED EZER
www.odedezer.com

HENDERSONBROMSTEADART
www.hendersonbromsteadart.com

FONS HICKMANN M23
www.fonshickmann.com

MORGAN GUEGAN
www.morganguegan.com

HATCH DESIGN
www.hatchsf.com

JAMES HEIMER
www.jamesheimer.com

ZACH HOBBS
zach@trueblue.us

INVISIBLE CREATURE
www.invisiblecreature.com

JEWBOY CORPORATION
www.jewboy.co.il

KWERTY
www.flickr.com/oldirtmckwert

LEDOUXVILLE
www.ledouxville.com

YANN LEGENDRE
www.legendrerutter.com

RON LIBERTI
ronliberti@hotmail.com

THE LITTLE FRIENDS OF PRINTMAKING
www.thelittlefriendsofprintmaking.com

LOVELY MPLS
www.lovelympls.com

ELLEN LUPTON
www.designwritingresearch.org

MODERN DOG
www.moderndog.com

MORNING BREATH, INC.
www.morningbreathinc.com

MOUNT PLEASANT
www.itsmountpleasant.com

NATHANIEL MURPHY
www.nathanielmurphy.com

THE NEW YEAR
www.thisisthenewyear.com

GUILLAUME NINOVE
www.guillameninove.com

NOTHING: SOMETHING: NY
www.nothingsomething.com

PATENT PENDING DESIGN
www.thepatentpending.com

AXEL PEEMOELLER
www.de-war.de

SAGMEISTER, INC.
www.sagmeister.com

SANDSTROM DESIGN
www.sandstrompartners.com

NATALIE SCHAEFER DESIGN
www.natalieschaefer.com

DENNY SCHMICKLE DESIGN
www.dennyschmickle.com

SERIPOP
www.seripop.com

THE SMALL STAKES
www.thesmallstakes.com

SOMMESE DESIGN
lxs14@psu.edu

SUB POP RECORDS
www.subpop.com

SUSSNER DESIGN CO.
www.sussner.com

THINKMULE
www.thinkmule.com

TRIP PRINT PRESS
www.tripprintpress.ca

UNDERCONSIDERATION
www.underconsideration.com

JAY VOLLMAR
www.jayvollmar.com

WEATHERMAKER PRESS
www.weathermakerpress.com

JOANNA WECHT DESIGN
www.joannawecht.com

MARTIN WOODTLI
www.woodt.li

YOKOLAND
www.yokoland.com

ZITYPE WORKSHOP
www.zitype.com

About the Author

John Foster is a designer in Washington, D.C. as the Principal and Superintendent of Bad People Good Things LLC. He is the author of *For Sale: Over 200 Innovative Solutions in Packaging Design* (HOW Books), *New Masters of Poster Design* (Rockport), *Maximum Page Design* (HOW Books), as well as an upcoming monograph on the work of Jeff Kleinsmith for Sub Pop Records. He writes a weekly column on music packaging, "Judging a Cover by Its Cover," for brightestyoungthings.com, and he performs musically under the guise of Sad Crocodile. He is an international speaker on design issues and has appeared several times at the world's largest design gathering, the HOW Design Conference. His work has appeared in all of the major publications, and he is the proud recipient of a Gold Medal from the Art Directors Club of Metropolitan Washington and a Best in Show from the ADDYs. His work has been shown in galleries around the globe and is part of the Smithsonian's permanent collection. Foster resides in Maryland with his lovely wife and daughter and two of the world's goofiest foxhounds.

Additional Work from Bad People Good Things shown on pages 6-7 and 206-207:

Firm: Bad People Good Things

Title: Shake Your Booty Big Ass Sale

Designer: John Foster

Size: 18 x 24 inches (45.7 x 61 cm)

Materials: Pencil, Pen, Ink, Xerox, Dress pattern

Printing Process: Screenprint

Firm: Bad People Good Things

Title: Flin Flon at The Warhol Museum

Designer: John Foster

Size: 12 x 18 inches (30.5 x 45.7 cm)

Materials: Ink, Paint, Old comics, Xerox, Letraset type

Printing Process: Screenprint

Firm: Bad People Good Things

Title: Mountain Goats

Designer: John Foster

Size: 12 x 18 inches (30.5 x 45.7 cm)

Materials: Pencil, Pen, Ink, Xerox, Sears and Roebuck catalog

Printing Process: Screenprint

Firm: Bad People Good Things

Title: Melvins

Designer: John Foster

Size: 19 x 25 inches (48.3 x 63.5 cm)

Materials: Pencil, Pen, Ink, Xerox, Letraset type

Printing Process: Screenprint